ORGANIZATIONAL BEHAVIOUR IN ITS CONTEXT

Dedicated to
'our' organizations in particular
and organization theory in general

Organizational behaviour in its context

THE ASTON PROGRAMME III

Edited by
D.S. PUGH
*London Graduate School
of Business Studies*
R.L. PAYNE
*MRC Social and Applied
Psychology Unit
University of Sheffield*

SAXON HOUSE

301.183
O 6781

1 0001 000 038 519

174373

Published by
SAXON HOUSE, Teakfield Limited,
Westmead, Farnborough, Hants., England.

ISBN 0 566 00159 4
Library of Congress Catalog Card Number 76-50966
Printed in Great Britain by Biddles Ltd of Guildford

Contents

Introduction

This is the third volume of a series reporting work developed in the 'Aston Approach'. Volume I of the series (Pugh and Hickson, 1976) reported the original studies on comparative organizational structure and context carried out at the Industrial Administration Research Unit of the University of Aston in Birmingham during the 1960s. Volume II (Pugh and Hinings, 1976) reported later studies at Aston and elsewhere which replicated and extended the original work, using the approach with a wider range of concepts, and types of organizations (local government departments, colleges, churches and trade unions) and, in the case of business firms, examining the links of context and structure to economic performance. It is hoped that a further volume will report the cross-cultural studies conducted at the structural level.

The present volume presents studies which examine the relationships between organizational context and structure on the one hand, and aspects of group and role structure and individual attitudes and behaviour on the other. As the original programme statement of the Aston group put it: 'we are concerned with the attempt to generalize and develop the study of work organization and behaviour into a consideration of the interdependence of three conceptually distinct levels of analysis of behaviour in organizations: (a) organizational structure and functioning, (b) group composition and interaction, and (c) individual personality and behaviour. We are also concerned to interrelate each of these levels. Thus, for example, we aim to study a particular level of analysis, say group composition and interaction, systematically *in relation to* particular organization structures, not, as so often in the past, in neglect of them' (Pugh et al., 1963).

The intention in the present studies has been to use established relationships between environment, context, structure and performance at the organizational level of analysis as independent variables and to examine group and individual aspects as dependent variables within given organizational settings. Our aim is to develop theories which elucidate the differential impact that situational constraints (such as context and structure) have upon patterns of social relationships and behaviour.

The interrelationships of levels of analysis

In Figure I we present a framework from a systems point of view, which outlines the focus of the present studies and their relationship to those previously reported. The major units of analysis are the organization, departments or major segments of organizations, small groups or teams, and the individual.

In the diagram, the conversion process has been divided into 'aims and resources' and 'structure and processes' to emphasize that the behaviour which takes place and the attitudes which are developed are a result of an interaction between these two aspects. The behaviour and attitudes are a result of the attempt to achieve aims given the demands, opportunities and constraints of the environment in which the unit of analysis (the system) is functioning. There are two-way arrows linking the boxes marked 'aims and resources' and 'structure and processes' for we consider that the resources available tend to determine the structure and processes that occur, but that there is a continual interaction between these processes and the aims, tasks and the use to which resources are put.

The lists of variables in the boxes are not meant to be exhaustive, but to represent some of the major features that have been studied. Hopefully, Figure I also conveys the fact that individuals and groups are part of a larger system, and that the larger system forms part of the environment of these sub-systems. The dotted arrows down the left-hand side are intended to convey this. The research implication is highlighted by Katz and Kahn (1966): 'The first step [in research] should always be to go to the next higher level of system organization, to study the dependence of the system in question upon the super system of which it is a part, for the super system sets the limits of the variance of behaviour of the dependent systems.'

The dotted arrows up the right side of the diagram indicate that lower level systems also can have effects on the supra-systems. An individual in the form of a chief executive can have considerable effects on the structure and processes of the organization as a whole. This illustrates nicely the interdependence between the various systems within organizations and allows us to stress the need for explanations which combine structural, group, and individual frameworks.

Using this overall conceptual framework with its reciprocal feedback loops underlines our view (Pugh et al., 1963) that an understanding of organizational operation can rest solely neither on the explication of structural characteristics and constraints nor on the explication of the constrictions of the individual actors. Organizational theorists should

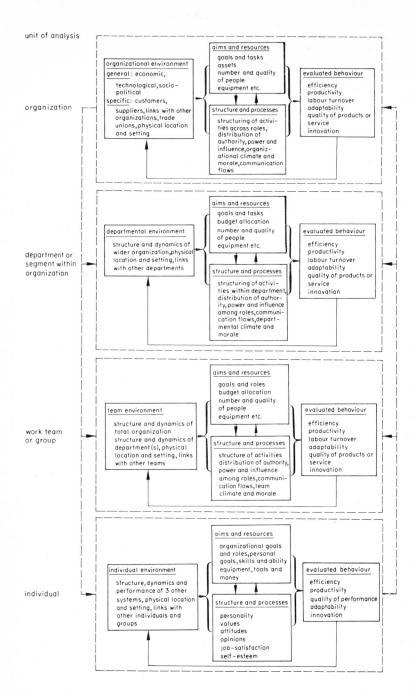

Fig. I   A framework for the study of behaviour in organizations
(adapted from Payne and Pugh, 1971)

concentrate on the interplays between them. Thus this approach is concerned both with system constraints and individual social action, attempting to bring them together in an overall framework (cf. Pugh and Hinings, 1976, pp. 175-6).

Objective and subjective measurement

The extension of the programme to group and individual level variables immediately raises the methodological question of 'objective' and 'subjective' approaches to data and measurement. The Aston approach to the study of organizational context, structure and performance has been a non-personal or objective one, in that there has been a direct assessment of organizational properties without any conceptual transformation. Here the organizational member is an *informant* about available measurement instruments. He is asked: 'What is the size of organization in terms of numbers of employees?', 'What are the standard procedures (if any) for inspecting the output?', 'What has been the percentage growth in net assets over the past five years?' Wherever possible documentary evidence is obtained to substantiate the verbal information given.

At the group and individual level of study, which is concerned with such concepts as role conflict, group cohesion and developmental climate, a 'subjective' approach has been used. Here it is the individual perceptions of the organizational member that are focused on, and he is a *respondent* to individual measurement instruments. He is asked: 'How precisely are your responsibilities laid down?' (a scale of responses from 'very precisely' to 'not at all'), 'New ideas are always being tried out here' ('strongly agree' to 'strongly disagree'). The responses are then aggregated to form role, group or organizational climate characteristics.

As Payne and Pugh (1976) have shown in their survey of the studies examining the relationships between structure and group and individual variables, the distinction between subjective and objective is not co-terminous with the distinction between, say, climate and structure. There have been several studies which obtain information on structure by subjective measurements (e.g. Hall, 1963; Hage and Aiken, 1967; Litwin and Stringer, 1968) or which obtain objective information on climate (e.g. Barker, 1965). But the link between objective–structural and subjective-role, group, climate studies has been characteristic of the studies reported here.

The use of subjective individually based data as a means of characterizing a social collectivity (e.g. a work-group, department, or organization) faces two important problems. The first is a conceptual one concerning the meaningfulness of aggregated measures; the second a methodological one concerning the validity of the methods of analysing relationships between aggregations.

In order to obtain a meaningful group property from subjective data, is a 'voting' procedure sufficient (e.g. taking the mean of individual responses) or is some high degree of consensus to be looked for? Pace (1963) suggests that two-thirds of the members should agree before the attribute should be considered a collective one; Guion (1973) proposes 90 per cent agreement. These would seem attractive criteria but how realistic are they with obtainable data? Would an approach using the mean be appropriate if it can be shown that the spread of responses (i.e. the standard deviation) was small relative to the possible range? Alternatively the use of the standard deviation itself as an additional and complementary index could be explored (as in Chapter 9).

Even when some, usually arbitrary, decision has been made on this issue, there remains the problem of interpreting correlations obtained between aggregate scores. It is known (Guilford, 1954) that correlations based on averages can produce misleading interpretations of the data. What adjustments can be made to improve the true estimates of the relationships between group characteristics? These issues, endemic to the study of subjective data in organizational research, recur throughout this volume, and current discussion of them is taken up in Chapter 10.

The plan of this volume

The three key concepts which we have used to organize the studies at the group and individual level of analysis are those of role, group and climate, which are presented in Parts I, II, and III respectively of this volume. In each case the concepts are related to the organizational level of analysis.

Part I, which is concerned with role, begins with a survey by Hickson (Chapter 1) of the use of this concept in organization theory. He suggests that there has been a considerable convergence in thinking and research on one particular aspect of the concept, namely the specificity (or precision) of role prescription and its obverse, the range of legitimate discretion. Three points emerge from his survey: (i) a linear relationship between degree of role prescription and other behavioural variables is almost universally taken for granted, (ii) relatively little work had been done to devise measures of role prescription, (iii) unless awareness of this convergence in thinking is increased, development may be inhibited. This paper (published in 1966) provided the starting point for the Aston studies at the group and individual level.

Chapter 2 (by Inkson, Hickson and Pugh) presents the first attempt to examine the relationships between aspects of organizational context and structure and aspects of the subjective experience of their roles by a group of top managers in organizations. It is a first test of 'the administrative reduction of variance' thesis, i.e. that a greater degree of organizational structuring as defined by Pugh et al. (1968) will be accompanied by an equivalent reduction of variability in managerial role behaviour as evidenced by increased role routine and definition, and decreased innovative role-sending and interpersonal conflict. In Chapter 3, Child presents a replication on a larger scale as part of the 'National Study' which examines the same variables. From the same study, Ellis and Child, in Chapter 4, relate some role and individual aspects of managers to their orientations towards behaviour at work, and compare these with some socially held behavioural stereotypes.

Part II of this volume focuses on the functioning of groups within the organizational structure. From a detailed study of all the levels of management in two structurally different organizations, Pheysey, Payne and Pugh examine interrelationships between the composition, structure and climate of the groups, and the organizational structure which are presented in Chapters 5 and 6.

Part III deals with the relatively newer concept of 'organizational climate', which is concerned with individuals' perceptions of the way the organization works, and the norms and values implicit in the behaviour of members. Tagiuri's (1968) definition serves as a starting point: 'Organizational climate is a relatively enduring quality of the internal environment of an organization that (a) is experienced by its members, (b) influences their behaviour, and (c) can be described in terms of the values of a particular set of characteristics (or attributes) of the organization.'

As Payne and Pugh (1976) show in their survey of studies of climate, several questionnaires had been designed to measure climate by 1968, and the major dimensions they produced were summarized by Campbell et al. (1970) as: (i) individual autonomy, (ii) degree of structure imposed on the position, (iii) reward orientation and (iv) consideration, warmth and support. The similarity between the first two climate dimensions and the Aston dimensions of centralization and structuring of activities is striking, and was emphasized by Campbell and his colleagues. It forms an encouraging link between the two levels of analysis, and has provided convergent validity of both types of measures.

The studies in Part III describe the developments by Payne and Pheysey (Chapter 7) of a measure of climate appropriate to business organizations, which they then use to explore relationships to contextual and structural features. Chapters 8 and 9 by Payne and Mansfield report a further and larger study of these relationships, which also explores in detail the effects of hierarchical position on an individual's perception of climate.

The final chapter (Concluding remarks) reviews the results obtained from the reported studies, and considers how far our understanding of behaviour in organizations has been developed at this level, and how well the links have been forged with the structural and contextual attributes of organizations.

The research team process: a view from the third generation (R.L. Payne)

The first two volumes included short descriptions of the institutional arrangements and historical factors which enabled the Aston studies to continue over a period of ten years whilst the research personnel involved went through three generations. The third generation consisted of Diana Pheysey, Kerr Inkson and myself, who joined the Unit in 1965, and John Child and Will McQuillan, who came somewhat later. Derek Pugh and David Hickson remained to provide the direction, wisdom and socialization that befalls grandparents in the extended nuclear family. And the view I wish to take is that of the group as a family. It was Jennifer Platt who, having interviewed several of the Aston group for her research into research (Platt, 1976), observed that the Unit sounded like a total institution. That is a caricature but it was certainly different from any of the other research groups that I have been in.

What struck me as a newcomer was the clarity of the philosophy that Pugh and Hickson had about how to run the group and the amount of time and energy they spent in making that philosophy live. Their efforts were directed towards four areas: the research itself, social relations in the group, social relations outside work itself, and the Unit's relations with the wider University.

It was suggested in Volume II that the second generation of Aston researchers had not sustained their interest in the Aston research because they had not been party to the design and conceptual development of the project, but had arrived to work on other people's research. The third generation had arrived to relate the organization measures to economic performance and to groups in organizations and this was virgin territory. Thus they had a common goal which they helped to design. At the same time we also got deeply involved with the final stages of analysis of the organizational data. Pugh and Hickson observed in Volume I that 'it is possible to look back and say that conceptualization and measurement of variable X was due more to researcher Y than to anyone else, but it is not possible to say that any particular bit of the work belonged to any one person'. Thus I can look back and say Diana Pheysey had a lot to do with technology and dependence, Kerr Inkson with the factor analysis of standardization, and I with 'status of specialisms'. This last never saw the light of day, but the identification with bits of the work and the contact with all of it served very well to socialize us into the Aston approach to organizations and all the third generation researchers have published work about this level as well as about roles and groups.

It was not only the common goal that helped to socialize us, but the way we were involved. Even though the project was very advanced we were involved in discussions about past and present ideas and actively encouraged to try our ideas on their data, though it very soon became known as 'our' data. This process was accelerated by the environment chosen by Pugh and Hickson. We all worked in one large room, including the secretary and the information/data assistants. This principle became more or less sacrosanct. During the four years I was at Aston, the total institution of the IARU was moved four times. Each time the principle of the large room was maintained, though each time the extra accommodation for private study etc. got better and better. The moves indicate the peripheral status of the research unit in a teaching institution, but the improvements in our accommodation also exemplify the political activity that was required to sustain, protect and develop the group.

Another event designed to improve our public relations also helped to accelerate the third generation's socialization. A few months after our arrival, the chief executives of the fifty-two organizations which had participated in the first study were invited to the University to hear about the research. It was a whole day affair, opened by the Vice Chancellor, Sir Peter Venables, invitations on gilt edged cards, pre-prepared press releases and all. And we quickly learned to say 'we did' in our rehearsed presentations, not 'they did'.

The processes behind outside/inside relationships also intermingled within the group itself. Relationships within the task group were encouraged through the 'Unit Fund'. This fund was financed from the payments for lectures, articles, talks, and the excess one made from field visits. The excess arose from the bureaucratic rules that allowed/sanctioned/forced you to collect what you were entitled to rather than what you actually spent. It was used to buy our own coffee percolator and crockery so that we had a continual supply of good coffee, drunk from good quality cups by us and visitors, many of whom were influential in the department. It was also used for Unit Christmas lunches, etc. It helped to support Unit family picnics, parties and car rallies, all of which helped to integrate wives into the 'family'. It has even been said that it was compulsory to live on the south side of Birmingham, but that is not true because two members did not – although I have the suspicion that Derek Pugh was never really happy about this!

It would be wrong to give the impression that commitment was total, because the involvement of families was regular but not frequent. It is a reflection of the commitment to the group though, since it indicates the time everybody put into social maintenance. Pugh and Hickson put in the most of course, but the point of this brief description is to emphasize that the continuance of the Unit over time demanded the commitment of time and energy to both task and socio-emotional activities. It seems to me that none of the subsequent attempts by various members of the Aston group to re-create these conditions has really been successful to the same degree. For that reason alone the events seem worth chronicling.

Acknowledgements

We should like to acknowledge the help which the authors of the papers presented here have received. In addition to comments from fellow contributors, earlier drafts of certain papers benefited from the comments of Colin Fletcher and Bob Hinings. Will McQuillan, Andrew Life, Bob Ashall and David Sutton contributed to the data collection of the 'National Study', parts of which are reported in Chapters 3 and 4. John Fairhead contributed to the data collection of the study reported in Chapter 8. Patricia Clarke and Ruth Goodkin contributed to the data analysis of the studies reported in Parts II and III.

The studies described in Chapters 2, 5, 6 and 7 were directly supported by the University of Aston through the provision of research posts. The 'National Study' (Chapters 3 and 4) was conducted at Aston and the London Business School and was supported by the Social Science Research Council, as was the study in Chapter 8 which was carried out at the London Business School.

In the compilation of this volume we are grateful to the Journals *Administrative Science Quarterly, European Journal of Social Psychology, Journal of Management Studies* and *Organizational Behaviour and Human Performance,* where the papers first appeared, for permission to reprint them.

The publisher's editorial task involved in the publication of compilations such as the present volume and the two previous ones in the series is inevitably heavier than usual. We are extremely grateful to our publishers – in particular John Irwin and Katie Lewis – for their help and forbearance. At the London Business School, Kay Schraer acted as our link (and filter!) with the publishers, gave her usual efficient secretarial help, and collated the bibliography. Eric Walton compiled the index. We are most grateful to all.

Derek Pugh   Roy Payne

London and Sheffield
October 1976

PART I

ROLE STUDIES

1 A convergence in organization theory*

D.J. HICKSON

In the cycles of investigation and speculation, the plethora of theories sometimes converges, and an underlying similarity in concept emerges from the varied terminologies. It may well be true that in diversity lies innovation. But when diversity is more in jargon than in ideas, research time is wasted before the common base is discovered, and what purports to be a lively range of exploration may disguise a general restriction within the bounds of one limiting perception. Such a convergence can be seen in the approaches of leading students to the structure of organizations.

Theory has converged upon the specificity (or precision) of role prescription and its obverse, the range of legitimate discretion. As Levinson (1959) writes, in his authoritative review of role theory, 'It is important also to consider the specificity or narrowness with which the normative requirements are defined. Norms have an "ought" quality; they confer legitimacy and reward value upon certain modes of action, thought, and emotion, while condemning others. But there are degrees here. Normative evaluations cover a spectrum from "strongly required" through various degrees of qualitative kinds of "acceptable," to the more or less stringently tabooed. Organizations differ in the width of the intermediate range on this spectrum. That is, they differ in the number and kinds of adaptation that are normatively acceptable. The wider the range – the less specific the norms – the greater is the area of personal choice for the individual.' There is nothing remarkable in pinpointing role theory here. Role is often cited as *the* link between social structure and personality, and as such must be central to organization theory. But to repeat Levinson's crushing comment: 'The concept of role remains one of the most overworked and underdeveloped in the social sciences.'

Of course, to use the very concept of role assumes a minimum prescription of organizational behaviour. Even the untrammelled research fellow who is said to have complete freedom of choice must select *some* pursuits that qualify as academic; even if he can go so far as to set up his

---

* originally published in *Administrative Science Quarterly,* vol. 11, 1966, pp. 225–37.

own business, he cannot devote himself to it exclusively without some accommodation to his role in the academic organization. So the specificity dimension runs from such roles, where prescription is in general terms and goes no further than outlining the boundaries of legitimate discretion, to roles where all but a fraction of role behaviour is minutely prescribed. Somewhere near the latter extreme comes the semiskilled assembly-line operator, as well as particular activities in the performance of some roles, for example, the first violin player when on stage. Thus, a role may extend over a range of this dimension.

If roles vary in specificity of prescription, who are the prescribers? The commonly accepted assumption is that structure embodies the prescriptions of the organization in general and of hierarchical superordinates (bosses) in particular.

Concepts of principal students

The concepts of some principal students of organization structure can now be examined. Their terminologies for the specificity of role prescription are presented in Table 1.1. In this table the contrast is drawn between high*er* and low*er* specificity, since it is not intended to imply that all the forms of structure discussed are at exactly high or exactly low positions on the continuum. Presumably they range along it, but there is a strong bimodal tendency in what many authors have written.

Structure analysts

Structure analysts from among sociologists and administration theorists have produced a varied list of terms. To begin with Weber's (1947) three ideal types, the structural accompaniments or consequences of the authority source are most elaborated for the rational-legal case. The features of a bureaucratic structure based on rational-legal authority do not need reiteration; this type shows highly specific prescription, as has been accepted by the many researchers and theorists who have used the concept of bureaucracy, and who therefore may be grouped anonymously under Weber's name. The traditionalistic or patriarchal structure can also be routinized to some extent, but a structure based on charisma suggests much lower specificity. Certainly Burns and Stalker (1961) see it that way. They find bureaucratic structure to be 'mechanistic', in that it does not easily adapt to technical and market change because of its 'precise definition of rights and obligations and technical methods attached to

4

Table 1.1
The terminologies used by various students of organization structure for specificity of role prescription

Students of organization structure	Terminologies for specificity (or precision) of role prescription	
	Higher specificity	Lower specificity
Structure analysts (Sociologists and administration theorists)		
Weber	Traditionalistic, bureaucratic	Charismatic
Burns and Stalker	Mechanistic	Organic (or organismic)
Barnes	Closed system	Open system
Whyte	Formalized	Flexible
Hage	High formalization (standardization)	Low formalization
Crozier	Routinized	Uncertain
Gordon and Becker	Specified procedures	Unspecified
Thompson	Overspecification	Structural looseness
Litwak	Weberian	Human relations
Janowitz	Domination: manipulation	Fraternal
Frank	Well-defined (and overdefined)	Underdefined
Simon	Programmed	Nonprogrammed
Presthus	Structured perceptual field	Unstructured
Bennis	Habit	Problem-solving
Structure designers (Management writers)		
Taylor	Scientific task determination	Personal rule-of-thumb
Fayol Urwick Brech	Clear statement of responsibilities	Personalities predominant (rather than intended design)
Brown	Explicit authority and accountability	Undefined roles and relationships
Structure critics (Social psychologists)		
Likert	Authoritative	Participative
McGregor	Theory X	Theory Y
Argyris	Rational organization	Self-actualization

each functional role'. They contrast it with the 'organic' form, later called 'organismic' by Burns (1963), in which role definitions are more general and continually change in interaction. Barnes' (1960) study of two engineering groups has produced strikingly similar results. He defines 'open' (as opposed to 'closed') organizational systems by high member autonomy, opportunities for interaction beyond the immediate task, and mutual influence across status levels. This same difference between 'formalized' and 'flexible' structures was noted years before by W.F. Whyte (1948). Hage's (1965) synthesis of organizational variables to formulate an axiomatic theory employs Burns and Stalker's terms, 'mechanistic' and 'organic', and contrasts high and low formalization (standardization); i.e. 'the proportion of codified jobs and the range of variation that is tolerated within the rules defining the jobs'.

Crozier (1964), tracing the patterns of power in organizations and building a 'strategic model' of group behaviour, relates power to the degrees of either structural routinization or uncertainty; routinization removes power, uncertainty gives scope for power. Hence, Crozier attributes the power of the maintenance engineers in the 'industrial monopoly' he studied to their control of machines; i.e. 'Control over the last source of uncertainty remaining in a completely routinized organizational system'. Likewise, Burns and Stalker find political conflict surrounding research and development units, which are relatively organismic, when they are introduced into mechanistic structures. The shift of power within hospitals from physicians to administrators is yet another example, according to Gordon and Becker (1964), who attribute it to modern medical techniques. These enable administrators to specify the procedures and resources to be used in treatment. Specified procedures improve administrative coordination, but mounting conflict may be anticipated as physicians defend their discretionary prerogatives against the encroaching rules.

Thompson (1965) suspects 'overspecification' of human resources of preventing innovation, whereas 'structural looseness' implies dispersion of power and therefore the forcing of more alternative solutions to those problems in which 'power meets power'. Searching for models of complex organizations that permit such conflict, Litwak (1961) compares three models: the Weberian, the human relations, and the professional, which differ in the extent of 'a priori specification of job authority' and 'hierarchical authority'. Likewise, Janowitz (1959) contends that under the impact of new weapons, military authority is changing from the 'domination' of explicit instruction to 'manipulation', with a possible further adaptation to a 'fraternal type' system, a trend he sees also in

6

non-military organizations.

Some analysts have used a more psychological frame of reference. Foremost among them is Simon (1960) with his well-known 'programmed-nonprogrammed' continuum. This computer analogy is colourful, but may have obscured the connection with organization structure. Fortunately, Burns and Stalker forge a link by associating nonprogrammed decision making with what they call organismic systems. Simon also records what has been dubbed 'Gresham's Law of Planning'; i.e. 'that programmed activity tends to drive out nonprogrammed activity' from a job. Here is a second direct link with the sociological point of view, for it complements Crozier's hypothesis about power. To Simon, increasing the routinization of the area of activity controlled by an executive implies that his attention will be increasingly held by programmed decisions to the neglect of nonprogrammed decisions; to Crozier, increasing routinization implies a loss of power. Thus, programmed decisions go with a lack of power, and nonprogrammed decisions go with power (as Gordon and Becker's hospital physicians are discovering). Presthus (1958), like Simon, derives his hypotheses from the psychological end of the spectrum. According to Presthus, precise definition of status and role gives clear perceptual cues, i.e. a highly 'structured field'. He uses Sullivan's (1953) formulation of the theory of 'anxiety reduction' as basic social motivation to suggest that the structuring of the perceptual field is inversely related to anxiety. People try to reduce anxiety by more clearly defining the social organization. This, too, agrees with Burns and Stalker, who, though proposing an organismic structure as suited to present-day dynamic conditions, do not claim that all is bliss in such an organization; the uncertainty in a flexible structure where a person does not know what he or the other fellow is supposed to be doing brings stress and strain as well as innovation. It is a symptom of what Bennis (1959) calls a 'problem-solving organization' as distinct from a 'habit organization'.

Structure designers

Specificity of role prescription also preoccupies management writers on the design of organizations. Leading this group is Taylor (1947) advocating detailed task prescription based on 'scientific' investigation instead of rule-of-thumb methods. Fayol (1949) emphasizes control and coordination through a clear line of command and specification of responsibility, and this argument is carried forward by Urwick (1947) and his associate Brech (1957). Urwick's 'Principle of Definition' states that the responsibilities of each position and its relationships with other positions should be defined in writing and made known to everyone concerned. Similarly, Brown (1960) divides the organization into an 'Executive System', a 'Representative System', and a 'Legislative System'; and then urges a careful analysis of roles and role relationships so that prescriptions can be clear, and confusion avoided.

Structure critics

Social psychologists have ranged themselves as critics of rational structure for the narrow limits it puts on group and individual autonomy. They have contended, however, that even with the high specificity of role prescription that it entails, there is sufficient discretion remaining in each superordinate role to allow leaders to ameliorate the effects of this specificity upon subordinate motivation and attitudes. In doing so, leaders may modify the role prescription itself. Impressive evidence has been marshalled by Likert (1961) in favour of increasing subordinate participation; that is, reducing the specificity of role prescription by allowing employees more control of the details of their own tasks. He compares the 'job-organization system of management' developed where repetitive work predominates, which stresses complete prescription of performance and tight control standards, with the 'cooperative-motivation system' intuitively used for more varied work, which leaves much more to the motivation of the employee. This analysis leads Likert to advocate an employee-centred rather than a job-centred style of supervision; and he puts forward a tabulation of the organizational and performance characteristics of 'Authoritative' as against 'Participative' management systems. Very much in the same mould is McGregor's (1960) crystallization of Theory X and Theory Y as opposing assumptions about motivation, leading respectively to coercion and direction of the employee or to increasing self-control and self-direction.

Argyris (1960) holds that, in Western society, individuals need to develop along seven psychological continua toward greater self-actualization and maturity, a development which the design and management of rational organization frustrates. He too notes (Argyris, 1964) the convergence of ideas of a number of students upon a mechanistic-organic distinction in organization.

Curvilinear relationships?

All the writers mentioned appear to accept the hypothesis of a linear relationship between precision of role prescription and whatever other behaviour variables interest them; as, for example, innovation of ideas, volume of output, job satisfaction, and so on. The curvilinear hypothesis should not be ignored, however. It may be held, for example, that even where output and employee participation are directly related, output will not continue to respond indefinitely to more participation, that is, to decreasing prescription. Perhaps the anxiety brought by participating in responsibility eventually outweighs the motivational benefits. At the other extreme, increasing prescription may go beyond the point where it succeeds in circumscribing behaviour, to a point where so much is explicitly required that it cannot all be done, and individuals must again live on their wits in the resulting confusion. Frank (1963) advances this latter hypothesis when he contrasts (1) 'Underdefined' administrative roles, (2) 'Well-defined' administrative roles, and (3) 'Overdefined' roles. *Both* the first and third permit *more* discretion than the second; for in 'Overdefined' roles expectations are so excessive or so conflicting that people are compelled to innovate in order to 'satisfice' (as Simon puts it).

Concomitants of role specificity

Although these various students are all concerned with the role specificity of organization structure, the variables they have chosen to relate to the degree of specificity are several and different, as Table 1.2 shows, and there is no consensus on relationships with organizational and individual performance.

Table 1.2
Comcomitants of specificity of role prescription

Higher specificity	Lower specificity			
Reduces confusion	More motivating	More innovating	Result: anxiety	Result: power conflict
Taylor	Likert	Burns and	Presthus	Crozier
Fayol	McGregor	Stalker	Burns and	Gordon and
Urwick	Argyris	Thompson	Stalker	Becker
Brech	Barnes	Frank		Litwak
Brown	(Bennis)	Bennis		
Weber		Hage		

Among the management writers there is comparative unanimity that clear lines of authority and responsibility are desirable, as is clear role definition. Then people can get on with their jobs without confusion, and performance will improve. This is the case for *higher* specificity. In arguing it, Taylor, Fayol, Urwick, Brech, and Brown find themselves an ally in Weber. Almost alone amongst sociologists, Weber regards the calculability of behaviour in organizations with high specificity (bureaucracies) as affording them a superiority in operation that overrides the dysfunctions so often pointed out by subsequent writers.

Likert, McGregor, and Argyris, however, are led by the findings of social psychology to take a critical view of rational structure. Explicitly, or by implication, they prefer *lower* specificity where individual self-realization, job commitment, and job satisfaction may be raised, and performance too. Barnes agrees; for in his study the 'open system' seemed to show greater personal autonomy and better results than the 'closed system'. Bennis cautiously refrains from evaluation, but contrasts the leadership function in the two settings in a way which accords with the social psychologists. It is a contrast between leadership in enforcing performance criteria and leadership in fostering conditions under which individual and organizational goals become congruent.

Others have hypothesized an inverse relationship between specificity, and technical and structural innovation. This is a severe qualification of the position taken by the management group of writers. Burns and Stalker, Thompson, Frank, Bennis, and Hage, when considering 'adaptiveness', all expect greater innovation when specificity is lower. (Frank also predicts innovation at the other extreme of overdefinition, when role incumbents are forced to use personal initiative in deciding which definitions to fulfil and which to neglect.)

However, lower role specificity can bring anxiety as Presthus, and Burns and Stalker, suggest, because the individual is not able to rely on detailed direction from above. Likewise, though it may bring more power to a role, as Crozier, and Gordon and Becker, hypothesize, it thereby confers the power to engage in conflicts over the distribution of power. So these authors, and Litwak, associate lower specificity with conflict between roles that have differing degrees of specificity, conflict about the extension of rules and procedures, which may increase the power of those making the rules and decrease the power of those subject to the rules.

A developmental trend in organization structure has been envisaged by several writers, going beyond the contemporary bureaucratic level of specificity to a lower level. Burns and Stalker's 'organic' form is a coming stage more suited to the future rate of innovation, as is Janowitz's 'fraternal type'. Argyris goes so far as to suggest that organizations may be able to arrange that roles have differing levels of specificity for differing areas of decision and activity, so that the structure can be varied according to the type of decision faced. In effect, there will be a different organization chart for each type of decision. Rather similarly, Whyte notices the possibility of an organization where relations are flexible when decisions are being discussed, but decisions are made through well-defined channels. Simon looks to electronic data processing to replace such channels and to replace clerical routines as means of gathering information for decisions. Judgement and intuition can then give way to 'heuristic problem-solving techniques', but in a more centralized structure.

Grouping writers by the variables they have associated with role specificity draws attention to other ranges of variables where little or nothing has been done; for example, small-group formation in organizations, and small-group processes from sociometric choice to tension-release mechanisms. It could be asked whether there are more groups per organization if specificity is lower: Are they smaller? Are they more cohesive? Do they show more tension? And so on. Nor have possible relationships been tested with personality traits, attitudes, or ways of thinking. For example, does not organizational innovation presuppose individual creativity? If so, then the low specificity associated with innovation must also be related to creativity. But, in addition, it is hypothesized that low specificity is related to anxiety and to power conflict. Drawing these several hypotheses together, if innovation is associated with low specificity, then the underlying individual creativity must not only survive conditions of anxiety and power conflict but even derive stimulation from them. Can this be tested in the field in organizations?

Conclusions

What is now apparent is the need not only for the integration offered by a concept such as specificity of role prescription, but for means of measuring variations of structure along this common dimension. If theory is so overwhelmingly focused, then measurements of degree of specificity are needed, first to verify the variations discerned by general observation, second to test hypotheses about the kinds of organization in which differing specificities occur, and third to test hypotheses relating group and individual variables to structure. Measurement may also help to rid us of hypothetical conundrums such as: Which is the more prescribed, a role where the area of discretion is specified precisely, or a role where, although the area of descretion may be less, exactly what it is remains rather vague? Could the idea of a bureaucratic–mechanistic–closed–formalized–routinized–specified–dominant–well-defined–programmed–perceptually structured–habit–'scientific'–authoritative–rational structure be condensed into a prescription-specificity score? This might offer simplicity where, before, the profusion of terminology swamped the student.

The measurers are few, hardly any. Kahn et al. (1964) in their major work on organizational stress measure role conflict, and role ambiguity ('the degree to which required information is available'), and this must encourage all who follow them; but they treat 'the prescriptions and proscriptions associated with a particular position' as a given rather than as a variable to be measured. Gross et al. (1958) do just touch on specificity with their initiative scale for school superintendents, which assesses how closely superintendents should adhere to the specific prescription of school committee rules. But it is Jaques (1961) who is ahead here. He has long distinguished the 'prescribed' from the 'discretionary' work content of roles, and proposes as a measure the time-span of discretion; i.e. 'the period of time during which marginally substandard discretion could be exercised in a role before information about the accumulating substandard work would become available to the manager in charge of the role'. Successful development of his technique and its widespread use may offer the best chance of profiting from the convergence of theory. A very limited trial of a comparatively crude scale of discretion is reported by Kammerer (1964), who assesses the degree of discretion permitted to American city managers on each of a range of topics.

Also, Pugh, the author, and other researchers (Pugh et al., 1963) are attempting to devise measures of several dimensions of organization structure, including standardization (of procedures), formalization (amount of paperwork), and centralization (of decisions). Since a procedure forms part of the specific prescriptions of many roles and may be more highly specific if committed to writing, and since it may be unalterable except by higher decision, such measures are likely to be relevant to role specificity. Scales have been tested which, however rudimentary they may seem when published, may provide a starting point for other researchers. Certainly the potential integration demands progress in methods and accompanying operational definitions that will discriminate more subtly than gross characterizations, which tend to obscure convergence in theories.

12

Finally, it is disconcerting that so much thinking has been and is patterned by the same conceptual dimension, wittingly or unwittingly. There are available, even now, other dimensions of roles in organization structures which might be used to differentiate organizations. For example, Gross et al. (1958) have isolated the direction or sign of expectations (prescriptive or proscriptive) and their particularity (pertaining to a particular role or to many); Kahn et al. (1964) have measured role pressures (influence), role ambiguity, and several normative dimensions. Both groups of researchers have studied role conflict. Why should not research distinguish organizations by their degree of role particularity or role pressure, or role conflict, as well as by the customary role specificity? The convergence, if it be such, upon this concept should be recognized, in the hope that fresh ideas will be sought which are not just the same concept under yet another name.

2 Administrative reduction of variance in organization and behaviour: a comparative study*

J.H.K. INKSON, D.J. HICKSON and D.S. PUGH

This paper reports some results of a study of relationships between formal characteristics of organization structure and interpersonal and psychological characteristics.

To set the study in perspective, it is necessary to summarize previous work reported by the Industrial Administration Research Unit at the University of Aston (Pugh et al., 1963; Hickson and Macdonald, 1964; Hickson and Pugh, 1965; Inkson, Payne and Pugh, 1967; Hinings et al., 1967; Pugh et al., 1968; Pugh et al., 1969; collected in Pugh and Hickson, 1976). These papers reported the application of more than a hundred scales of organization to a sample of 46 diverse manufacturing and service organizations in the Midlands. A number of major underlying dimensions were put forward, supported by factor analysis. Among a wide range of 'contextual' variables potentially related to the forms taken by the formal structures of organizations, three stood out as salient in multivariate analyses. They are the organization's size, the workflow integration of its technology (measured by automaticity of equipment, rigidity of workflow sequence, etc.), and its dependence (on controlling groups of organizations and on suppliers, customers, etc.). A number of major stable dimensions of structure were put forward, supported by factor analysis: foremost were the degree of structuring of organizational activities and the degree of concentration of authority at the top of the organization. Strong and systematic relationships between organizational context and structure were demonstrated, structuring of activities being strongly related to size and moderately to workflow integration, and concentration of authority being strongly related to dependence.

---

* edited version of a paper originally presented to the Annual Conference of the British Psychological Society, 1968.

The present research was concerned to examine relationships between such organizational characteristics and the roles and behaviour of senior executive members of organizations. In particular, attention was focused on the effects of the two main structural dimensions, structuring of activities and concentration of authority. Structuring of activities is associated with a high degree of specialization of functions, standardization of procedures, and formalization of routines. A highly structured organization is likely, for example, to employ individuals full-time in specialist areas such as dealing with legal requirements, keeping stock records, and maintaining instruments, which would in an unstructured organization be performed by non-specialists with other duties; to have frequent and precise scheduling of work, planned maintenance, precise financial control procedures, standard formats for communication, and so on; and to have many areas of activity defined in terms of written documents such as job descriptions, manuals of procedures, programmes, agendas, reports, forms, and records. These features would seem to have the effect for the individual of limiting the range of activities which he may legitimately pursue as part of his job, and limiting the range of skills and practices he may use in performing these activities. The second factor, concentration of authority, would appear to imply similar effects. Since organizations high on this factor tend to locate authority to take decisions in the hands of an owning group, a board, or a chief executive, the discretion available to other members of the organization is likely to be limited, and the complexity of the decisions taken by them reduced.

This conception of the effects of structural factors has been elaborated by Hickson (see Chapter 1), who suggests that the work of a number of major organization theorists is linked by the single concept of 'specificity of role-prescription'. Further examination of this concept led us to believe that, conceptualized as an organic quality of the organization, it might provide a vital first step in establishing relationships between organizational and behavioural variables. It was hypothesized that the two main structural variables increase the degree of specificity of role-prescription characteristic of the organization, and that, in an environment thus formally defined in terms of highly prescribed roles, relatively cautious and conformist behaviour becomes most appropriate. Thus, in the role-sending activities described by Kahn et al. (1964), where formal roles are mediated by interpersonal role-conceptions and expectations, conformity and stability become highly valued. In this relatively stable organizational and social environment interpersonal conflict is less likely. Thus a single explanatory causal chain is hypothesized, whereby administrative factors in structured and/or concentrated authority

15

organizations reduce the amount of variance in roles, and thereby the amount of innovation and flexibility encouraged in interpersonal relations and conflict engendered by interpersonal behaviour. Organizational variables, role variables, and interpersonal variables are linked.

A strategy was accordingly developed for the testing of this chain of hypotheses. It was decided to study as large as possible a sample of organizations and to focus on senior executives in an attempt to obtain simply within each organization a sample of subjects representing a range of organizational functions. A questionnaire designed to assess subjective characterizations of role, behaviour, and interpersonal relationships was drafted, and, following a pilot study of thirty senior executives at a leading management college, revised. A further set of discrimination and factor analyses was carried out on the first 107 questionnaires returned in the study proper, which enabled conceptual dimensions to be further refined.

Of the variables assessed in the questionnaire, four in particular may be mentioned (see Figure 2.1). Two conceptually and empirically distinct aspects of specificity of role-prescription, suggested by a factor analysis of items representing sub-variables, were labelled Routine and Definition. Routine in a role is associated with the respondent reporting lack of change in tasks over time, few previously unencountered problems, little need for new techniques, and so on. Definition involves frequent set procedures, well-defined decisions and responsibilities, and so on. Each was assessed by the respondent in respect of the work-role set for him by the organization, using a six-item Likert-type scale for routine and a similar four-item scale for definition.

Among the interpersonal variables, Innovative Role-Sending was assessed by having each respondent complete a set of ten semantic

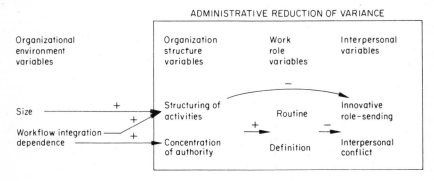

Fig. 2.1 Hypothesized relationships among variables of reduction of variance

16

differential-type scales describing how he thought other executives in his organization ought to act: examples of individual scales are 'questioning–complying', 'imaginative–down-to-earth', 'taking chances–playing safe'; the dimension underlying these scales had been established by prior factor analysis. Interpersonal Conflict was measured by asking respondents to complete a set of four rating scales describing the degree of difficulty senior managers normally had in reaching agreement over particular aspects of problems.

The overall characterization of each organization in terms of these role and interpersonal variables was established by taking the means of individual scores within each organization. We had some reservations about this procedure which, as Guilford (1956) points out, tends in homogeneous samples such as ours to inflate correlations between variables which are basically individual in character. However, all of the variables to which the procedure was applied made conceptual sense as whole organization characteristics. The work of Hall (1962) on bureaucratic characteristics and Hage and Aiken (1967) on structural properties of social welfare agencies may be cited as examples of such additive measures applied to organizational problems. In relation to these studies, however, it must be remembered that as we, unlike Hall and Hage, applied our procedures within the senior management sector only, the characterizations obtained are valid not of the organization as a whole, but of this sector only. This point has important implications in the light of our findings.

The method of investigation was as follows. The sample of organizations was drawn from a list of Birmingham organizations employing 250 or more, and was stratified according to size, so as to give approximately equal numbers of organizations in each of five size-bands: 250–500 employees; 501–1,000; 1,001–2,000; 2,001–5,000; and over 5,000. Altogether forty organizations participated. After the Chief Executive of each organization had agreed on behalf of the organization to participate in the project, an interview was arranged with them, or occasionally with his designated representative, to gather data on the context and formal structure of the organization. One problem was the time and labour required to collect data for the Unit's complete set of measures of organization. However, the high internal consistency of the main organizational dimensions suggested that these might be assessed accurately by a judicious selection of items and scales within them. Accordingly, a 'short' schedule was devised, designed to elicit the organization's scores on major dimensions in a single interview. This schedule included selected measures of workflow integration, dependence,

17

structuring of activities, and concentration of authority, which, when applied to the original data, all correlated 0·90 or better with full measures (cf. Inkson, Pugh and Hickson, 1970).

Interviews with Chief Executives averaged about an hour and a half in length. As well as gathering formal organizational data, these interviews involved identifying the main functional departments and heads on an organizational 'chart'. From this information a sample of senior executives was selected, which comprised all those who reported directly to the Chief Executive plus, if not thereby included, the heads of various designated specialist functions such as buying and personnel. Each individual thus selected was despatched a questionnaire plus a note indicating that the Chief Executive had agreed to the project. Altogether 326 questionnaires were sent out, an average of just over eight per organization, and 283 returned, a response rate of 87 per cent. Organizational means were computed on the basis of samples between three and eleven questionnaires per organization.

Some results are summarized in Table 2.1. Intercorrelations between the first five variables, those derived from the preceding study, are very similar to those obtained in that study. Again structuring of activities is

Table 2.1

Intercorrelations between nine organizational variables (decimal points omitted, n = 40 organizations)

	1	2	3	4	5	6	7	8	9
1 Size (no. of employees)		23	15	61†	11	—31*	—26	33*	—23
2 Workflow integration			—31*	51†	—39*	—44†	—43†	22	33*
3 Dépendence				17	66†	36*	19	11	—26
4 Structuring of activities					—24	—56†	—28	48†	08
5 Concentration of authority						22	16	—20	—34*
6 Routine							39*	—51†	—04
7 Definition								—16	—40†
8 Innovative role-sending									02
9 Interpersonal conflict									

†p ‹·01   * p ‹ ·05

chiefly associated with organizational size and workflow integration, concentration of authority with dependence.

To support the theoretical argument centred on specificity of role-prescription, we would expect structuring and concentration to be positively associated with routine and definition, and negatively with innovative role-sending and interpersonal conflict (Figure 2.1). But the results force a reappraisal of these hypotheses.

Innovative role-sending is indeed associated with organizational structuring of activities (beyond the 1 per cent level of confidence) – but positively, in the reverse direction to that predicted. Far from the executives of highly structured organizations expecting cautious, conformist, compliant behaviour of one another, they seek adaptability, innovation, and the taking of risks. This finding remains even when the effects of size and technology (workflow integration) are partialled out. At the same time, innovative role-sending is, as hypothesized, strongly negatively related to routine, which, surprisingly, is negatively related to organizational structuring. Thus, executives in highly structured organizations tend to experience less routine themselves, and to have mutual expectations of bold, innovative activities.

The surprising link between high structuring and innovative role-sending calls for explanation. At the moment we can only speculate. Possibly the explanation lies in the fact that our sample is confined to senior executives. It may be that in a very real sense these senior men are 'above' formal structuring of activities so that they are released from comparatively mundane tasks and can channel their energies into non-routine innovative activities. As measured, structuring may reflect an element of routinization of roles at levels 'lower' in the hierarchy. We would suggest that every organization has a 'gradient of routine' which represents differences in routineness of tasks according to level in the hierarchy. This gradient would be steeper in a highly structured than in a less structured organization, so that a study of operatives should show the reverse effects to those found among top managers. The hypothesis that structuring of activities is negatively related to innovative role-sending must therefore be applied over a range of levels of personnel, and cannot be considered to have been adequately tested on our present sample.

On the other hand, the chain of hypotheses does hold as predicted through from organizational concentration of authority to role routine and definition and to innovative role-sending, though most of the linking correlations are very low. There is some tendency for role-sending to be less innovative where authority is concentrated.

Interpersonal conflict is related to a very different mix of factors from that associated with innovative role-sending. Where lack of routine appears to be a dominant factor in the genesis of an innovative culture, conflict appears to be more closely associated with lack of definition. In organizations where executives perceive their responsibilities as being precisely laid down, they tend to find it easier to agree among themselves: where their responsibilities are less clear, conflict ensues.

Again, the original hypotheses suppose a relationship – a negative one – between the organizational level variable, structuring of activities, and the interpersonal variable, in this case conflict. Table 2.1 shows no such relationship. Nor is executive role definition associated with structuring in the way expected. Though other current analyses suggest that there may be complex relationships here among sub-variables, they are not strong. The link between structuring of activities and interpersonal conflict is not established, as far as executives are concerned. But there *is* some association between organizational concentration of authority and conflict, and also between size and technology of the organization, and conflict experienced. The results suggest that interpersonal conflict at the level of management under examination is greatest in small technologically sophisticated organizations where decision making is decentralized, probably to the respondent managers. Organizations at the other extreme, typically represented in our sample by local and central government service departments whose decisions are chiefly taken by governing bodies, and within which such responsibilities as exist are clearly defined, may leave their executives less to disagree over.

However, we hope we have been able to do enough to demonstrate effectively the validity of the point of view with which we started: 'A more accurate understanding of the behaviour of individuals and groups in organizations is surely attendant upon a more accurate description of the context in which the behaviour occurs, i.e., the organizational environment' (Inkson, Payne and Pugh, 1967, pp. 45–6). Full explanation in fact, depends on conceptualization and analysis at the levels of individual, group, and organization simultaneously.

3   Strategies of control and organizational behaviour*

JOHN CHILD

Introduction

The influence, both intended and unintended, which strategies of administrative control may have upon group and individual behaviour within organizations has been a subject of major interest in organization theory. There is disagreement as to whether bureaucratic administrative structures cause dependency and conformity (Merton, 1940; Argyris, 1957) or allow for self-direction and challenge (Porter, 1963; Kohn, 1971). Whichever view is taken, the debate points out the need to study simultaneously data at various levels of organizational analysis, examining relationships between variables located at different levels as well as those at the same level. Thus, as Inkson, Payne and Pugh point out, 'A more accurate understanding of the behaviour of individuals and groups in organizations is surely attendant upon a more accurate description of the context in which the behaviour occurs, that is, the organizational environment' (1967, pp. 45–6).

Inkson, Hickson and Pugh in a later paper (see Chapter 2) advanced the proposition that strategies of administrative control will influence modes of behaviour in organizations. They employed the concept of the administrative reduction of variance in behaviour in referring to the following series of hypothesized relationships between variables at different levels of the organization. First, the choice of organization structure was seen to reflect characteristics of the organization as a whole and of its operating rationale – what Pugh et al. (1969) have termed the context of organization structure. Second, Inkson and his colleagues postulated that two major strategies of administrative control, control through bureaucratization and control through centralized decision making, serve in different ways to limit descretion and to prescribe work roles. Third, the more the internal organizational environment is defined

---

* originally published in *Administrative Science Quarterly,* vol. 18, 1973, pp. 1–17.

in terms of highly prescribed roles, the more (it was argued) relatively cautious and conforming behaviour becomes appropriate. In this stable and controlled environment a high degree of conflict is also considered unlikely. The main hypothesized relationships contained in the administrative reduction of variance model are described in Figure 3.1.

As a framework within which empirical research can be conducted, the model of administrative reduction of variance in behaviour has several theoretical limitations. It postulates an asymmetrical set of causal influences running from organizational context to structure, to work role, to behaviour, influences which could be represented by systems of recursive equations. The causal theory contained in the model leans heavily towards the view that organization structure coerces people into a state of dependency and conformity, and it implies that behaviour in organizations can be understood largely in terms of intraorganizational rather than external conditions. It does not therefore allow for the possibility that the behaviour of individuals and groups within an organization may be intelligible in terms of exogenous factors shaping their expectations of work and career. Nor does it allow that organization members may to some extent themselves influence the structure of roles and administrative controls by imposing certain limits upon what is acceptable.

While these theoretical limitations have to be recognized, the model of administrative reduction of variance in behaviour nevertheless represents a significant advance towards analytical precision. Moreover, a mild interpretation of its underlying rationale, such that behaviour is seen to be constrained rather than determined by the organizational environment, is sufficiently acceptable to serve as a major, though not exclusive or exhaustive, theoretical perspective. The model will be used in this article to provide a general framework for distinguishing variables at different levels of organizational analysis and for exploring relationships between them. The source of data is a study of senior managers in seventy-eight British business organizations. Inkson, Hickson and Pugh (Chapter 2) have employed the same framework for reporting on another sample of British managers, and some comparison with their work is therefore possible.

Variables were classified according to four categories: organization context, organization structure, work role, and (interpersonal) behaviour. The definition of variables at the organization level, variables of structure and of context, is derived from the work of Pugh and his colleagues at the University of Aston. Four of their dimensions of organization structure (Pugh et al., 1968) have been incorporated into this study. All the

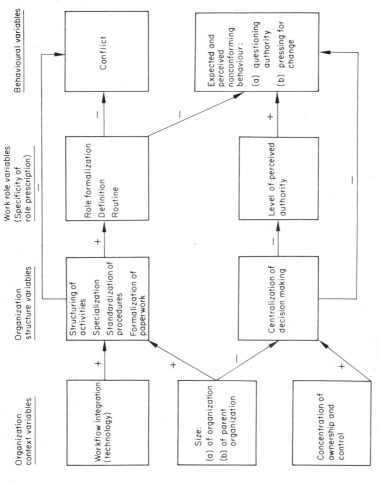

Fig. 3.1 Strategies of control and organizational behaviour: main hypothesized relationships (developed from Fig. 2.1).

23

dimensions refer explicitly to the definition and control of activity and behaviour within organizations.

Specialization, in the sense of functional specialization, is the extent to which official duties are divided between discrete identifiable functional areas. Specialization, in terms of role specialization, is the extent to which official duties are divided within functional areas between discrete identifiable positions. Standardization is the extent to which activities are subject to standard procedures and rules, while formalization is the extent to which procedures, rules, instructions, and communication are written down. Centralization is the extent to which the locus of authority to make decisions affecting the organization is confined to the higher levels of the hierarchy.

In addition to these structural variables, a subscale of formalization has also been included: recording of role performance. Although many of the items in this measure do not refer to managerial role performance, there is a presumption that role performance records – such as documents outlining work to be done, records of work completed, and so forth – will themselves act to define the roles of managers both in departments where role performance is being assessed and in departments which are carrying out the assessment.

The degrees of specialization, standardization, and formalization found empirically within organizations are closely related (Pugh et al., 1968; Child, 1972a). Pugh and his fellow researchers argued that high scores on these variables imply that an organization 'would have gone a long way in the regulation of the work of its employees. As an organization, it would have gone a long way in structuring its activities' (1968, p. 84). Centralization of decision making has been found to correlate negatively with the structuring variables, quite strongly so in manufacturing organizations. This is the basis for suggesting that, broadly speaking, there may be two alternative strategies of controlling organizational behaviour.

One may attempt to control behaviour indirectly by relying upon procedures and records as methods for limiting discretion (exception reporting is an example) and for monitoring activities. Within the limits imposed by such indirect controls, decisions can be delegated to lower levels in the hierarchy, and to employees in specialized roles, some of whom are concerned with operating the indirect control system itself. This can be termed the bureaucratic strategy of control. Or one may attempt to maintain control directly by confining decisions to fairly senior levels in the hierarchy. This economizes on the need for elaborate systems of procedures and paperwork. It may also reduce the need for certain areas of specialization such as those concerned with operating indirect control systems. This can be termed the centralizing strategy of control.

Variables of organization context are relevant in predicting the balance of choice between these strategies of administrative control. Thus, several comparative studies have found that size of organization is positively related to the structuring variables and negatively related to centralization of decision making (Pugh et al., 1969; Blau and Schoenherr, 1971; Child, 1972b). It seems likely that larger organization size sets up pressures towards a devolution of decision making within a framework of indirect controls which are designed to limit discretion to the area of events which are capable of being programmed. The results of one study (Child, 1972b) suggest that size of parent organizations is also associated with the degree of reliance on standardization and formalization; this is probably because (as field observation indicated) systems developed in large groups are often applied directly to a subsidiary organization. These studies also found a tendency for technological sophistication to be associated with a higher structuring of activities, while two of the three (Pugh et al.; Blau and Schoenherr) found advanced technology to be associated with decentralization of decision making. Finally, in data to be presented below, a greater concentration of ownership with control is found to correlate positively with a higher centralization of decision making within organizations.

These links between variables of context and those of structure have been incorporated into the framework of analysis presented in Figure 3.1. The four variables of organization context included are (1) workflow integration, which is a composite measure of technology referring to the rigidity in the sequence of an organization's various workflow patterns, the degree of automation of the equipment used, the technological integration between various operating segments, and the precision of inspection processes; (2) size of the organization, which is measured by the logarithm of total numbers employed; (3) size of parent organization which is the logarithm of total numbers employed by the group of which the organization studied may be a part or the whole; and (4) concentration of ownership and control, which is a composite measure referring to the concentration of vote-holdings, proportion of vote-holdings held by directors, and so forth.

The control effects of organization structure postulated by the administrative reduction of variance model have been crystallized by Hickson (Chapter 1) in his concept of specificity of role prescription. Hickson found in his review of the literature on organization theory that 'a linear relationship between the degree of role prescription and other

25

behaviour variables is almost universally taken for granted' (1966, p. 224). Treated as an organic quality of the organization, the concept of role prescription may therefore provide an important link in the establishment of relationships between organizational and behavioural variables. Developing this line of argument, Inkson et al. (1968) hypothesized that high values on the structuring variables (specialization, standardization and formalization) and a high degree of centralization serve to increase the specificity of role prescription characterizing the organization. Their argument is given in detail in Chapter 2 (p. 15).

Structuring of activities and centralization are, according to this argument, both expected to increase the specificity of role prescription characteristic of the organization, but in different ways. High values on the variables of structuring are postulated as resulting in roles being relatively formalized by official documents, relatively defined, and containing a large measure of routine activity. High centralization of decision making would be expected to reduce an organization member's level of authority in general. Strategies of administrative control are thus expected to reduce the amount of discretion in roles and in consequence the amount of innovative and nonconforming behaviour. In this relatively stable intraorganizational environment, reminiscent of Harrington's *Life in the "Crystal Palace"* (1960), it is hypothesized that conflict will be muted. In short, 'organizational variables, role variables and interpersonal variables are linked' (Inkson et al., Chapter 2).

Sample and method

Data on organizational variables will be presented for seventy-eight British business companies. These are the companies from a full sample of eighty-two organizations described by Child (1972a) where permission for a study of their managers was given. The companies were all located in six industries: advertising, chocolate and sugar confectionery, electronic instruments and components, insurance, daily newspapers, and pharmaceuticals. The measures of organization context and structure reported in this article have already been mentioned. Data for these measures were collected from chief executives and departmental managers using a standard interview schedule derived from investigations by Pugh et al. (1968).

Data on role and behavioural variables were collected from senior managers in the companies. For this managerial sample heads of department in thirteen specified functional areas were selected from each organization, together with any other managers (but not assistants) reporting directly to the chief executive. In some organizations the full range of functional managers was not present; in certain other organizations there were several heads of departments who would be categorized within a single function, such as several divisional production managers. The response rate for a postal questionnaire sent to these managers, between one and two weeks after completing the investigation of organizational variables, was 88·6 per cent. This response provided 787 usable returns.

For the analysis presented here an overall characterization in terms of role and behavioural variables was established for each organization's senior managerial group by taking the means of individual scores within the organization. These means were computed from samples of between three and twenty-five questionnaires per organization; normally, the larger the organization, the more managers came within the sampling frame. Some reservations can be expressed about this procedure which, as Guilford (1956) indicated, tended to inflate correlations between variables which are basically individual in character in relatively homogeneous samples such as this one.

On the other hand the justification for the procedure lies in the argument that the variables to which it was applied are conceptually acceptable as collective characteristics. The work of Hall (1962) on bureaucratic properties and of Hage and Aiken (1967) on structural properties of social welfare agencies can be cited as examples of such additive measures applied to organizational problems. Unlike those studies, however, the measures of role and behaviour used in the present research were applied only within the senior management sector. The characterizations obtained are therefore valid only for senior managers and not for the organization as a whole. While questionnaires were sent to managers in charge of all the major functional areas, the distribution of subjects by function for each organization does reflect the particular functional configuration of that organization's management team. A combination of this sampling with a high response rate allows for some confidence that aggregated scores are in fact representing each senior managerial group.

Data obtained from the questionnaires were used to construct measures of (1) perceptions of role characteristics (formalization, definition, routine, and authority), and (2) normative expectations and perceptions of behaviour (levels of questioning authority and pressing for change and perceived levels of conflict). These measures are described in Table 3.1, but it is necessary to comment further on how some of them were derived from the data.

Table 3.1
Summary of measures of managerial role and behavioural variables

	Name of variable	Nature of variable	Nature of measure	Sample item
1	***Work role variables***			
	1.1 Role formalization	Extent to which managers's role is formalized by prescription in official documents	Total of 5 biserial items	Is there a written job description or terms of reference for your job?
	1.2 Role definition	Extent to which managers perceive their jobs and authority to be constrained within fixed limits	Total of 3 weighted Likert-type (5-point) items	How precisely are your responsibilities laid down? (very precisely, fairly, not very, very imprecisely, not laid down at all)
	1.3 Role routine: problems and skills	Extent to which managers perceive their work as not involving unfamiliar problems or requiring new skills	Total of 5 weighted Likert-type (5-point) items	How often do completely unforeseen things happen in your job? (very often, often, sometimes, occasionally, seldom)
	1.4 Everyday routine	Extent to which managers perceive their work as involving little short term change	Total of 4 weighted Likert-type (5-point) items	How many of your working days follow a similar pattern to one another? (most, quite a lot, a few, almost none)
	1.5 Long-term stability	Extent to which managers perceive little change in their work year to year	Total of 2 unweighted Likert-type (5-point) items	How much of the content of the job you are now in has changed in the past year? (almost none, a little, some, quite a lot, most)
	1.6 Perceived authority	The scope of authority managers perceive themselves as possessing	Total of scores from two similar scales each describing 8 degrees of authority	I have complete authority on routine matters but refer the majority of unusual items to my superior for approval
2	***Behavioural variables***			
	Expected behaviour			
	2.1 Questioning authority	Extent to which a manager thinks his colleagues ought to question formal authority and rules	Total of 3 unweighted Osgood-type semantic differential items	Place a tick in one of the 7 spaces which most accurately describes how on the whole, managers should (do) carry out their tasks in the organization: accepting authority questioning authority : : : : : : :
	2.2 Pressing for change	Extent to which a manager thinks his colleagues ought to act innovatively and to accept corresponding risks	Total of 5 weighted Osgood-type semantic differential items	leaving well enough alone changing things : : : : : : :
	Perceived behaviour			
	2.3 Questioning authority	Extent to which a manager perceives his colleagues questioning formal authority and rules	as 2.1	accepting authority questioning authority : : : : : : :
	2.4 Pressing for change	Extent to which a manager perceives his colleagues acting innovatively and accepting corresponding risks	Total of 7 unweighted Osgood-type semantic differential items	using tried ideas trying new ideas : : : : : : :
	2.5 Conflict	Extent to which a manager perceives his colleagues finding difficulty in agreeing on four aspects of problem solving	Total of 4 Likert-type (5-point) items	How much difficulty do senior managers (in your organization) have in reaching agreement on the facts of the situation? (none, a little, some, quite a lot, a great deal).

Note: Variables 2.1 to 2.4 inclusive are conceptualized as nonconforming behaviour

An important part of the questionnaire was developed in order to operationalize the concept of specificity of role prescription. In a pilot study, fourteen Likert-type items were developed as central indicators of role prescription. A principal components analysis of responses by senior managers to these items revealed two main independent factors. These were labelled role routine and role definition. On the basis of this factor analysis Inkson et al. (1968) constructed a six-item measure for routine and a four-item measure for definition. The questionnaire used by Inkson et al. and in the present study was identical and it had been designed for use in both investigations. The data collected in the present study were also subject to principal components analysis, partly to investigate whether the previously found underlying structure could be repeated and partly as a general guide in the construction of measures. As it turned out, a more complex picture emerged than had been observed with the much smaller earlier samples; this is shown in Table 3.2.

Although none of the factors obtained are large in terms of variance

Table 3.2

Specificity of role prescription: principal components analysis
(varimax rotation) N = 787

Items (abbreviated from questionnaire and in rearranged order)	Factor I Routine nature of problems and skills		Factor II Role definition		Factor III Long-term stability	Factor IV Everyday routine	
		(Weighting)		(Weighting)			(Weighting)
Nothing completely unforeseen	78	(2·0)	03		07	14	
Few new problems	68	(1·5)	10		22	21	
No fresh skills required	68	(1·5)	—01		27	01	
Few switches of task	56	(1·0)	15		—16	07	
Solutions are clear	50	(1·0)	01			24	
Precisely defined responsibilities	03		87	(3·0)	06	07	
Precisely defined authority	05		86	(3·0)	04	05	
Much information on job description	13		45	(1·0)	—13	22	
Job content – little change in past year	08		—05		87	11	
Job content – little change expected over next year	13		04		86	06	
Much routine	14		10		06	77	(2·0)
Frequently follow set procedures	06		19		12	74	(2·0)
Days similar to one another	17		—01		13	71	(2·0)
Most foreseeable, week ahead	28		14		—19	47	(1·0)
Percentage of total variance	24·6		12·8		10·0	8·6	
Mean intercorrelation between the items marked	r = 0·31		r = 0·36		r = 0·63	r = 0·34	

Note: decimal points omitted.

accounted for, the analysis segregates the data in a manner which is conceptually acceptable. In particular it suggests the need to distinguish between three subcategories within the notion of role routine: (1) the routine character of problems encountered in regard to their intrinsic nature and to the skills required for their solution (Factor I); (2) an everyday aspect of routine much more at the level of work programming (Factor IV); and (3) long-term changes in a manager's job (Factor III). For purposes of the present study scores were computed for three types of routine and for role definition using the robust weightings shown in Table 3.2. The table also lists the items contained in these measures.

A similar procedure was adopted with two sets of eleven seven-point semantic differential items which respondents had been asked to score in regard to (a) how they thought managers at their level in the organization ought to behave and (b) what they perceived the normal behaviour of these managers actually to be. The items had all been included in the questionnaire as potential measures of nonconforming behaviour. Results of the principal components analysis suggested some differentiation between items which described the questioning of formal authority and rules and other items which gave a more general description of pressing for change. This differentiation was more clear-cut among the scores on perception of behaviour than among those on expected behaviour. The mean intercorrelation between the items of expected behaviour, however, were generally very low (mean r for all eleven items $= 0.24$). The particular factor solutions which were used as a guide to formulating measures from the items for expected and perceived behaviour are shown in Table 3.3. Scores for the items marked in Table 3.3 were aggregated, with the items in expected pressing for change (Factor A I) given weights as shown because their factor loadings were particularly dispersed in value. It was also decided not to include items 1 and 11 in the measure of expected questioning authority since they appeared conceptually somewhat removed from the notion of challenging authority and indeed were highly loaded on perceived pressing for change (Factor B I).

The scores for role formalization and for the level of conflict are the totals of constituent items. The mean intercorrelation between items for role formalization was $r = 0.27$ with a mean correlation of items with the total score of $r = 0.64$. For conflict the mean intercorrelation between items was $r = 0.44$ and the mean correlation of items with the total score was $r = 0.76$. These correlations are from the sample of 787 managers.

Comparison of the results obtained by Inkson et al. (1968) with those in the current study is possible only in broad terms. The earlier study employed a short form of organizational measurement derived from a

Table 3.3

Expected and perceived nonconforming behaviour: principal components analyses (varimax rotations) N = 787

Items	A Expected behaviour		B Perceived behaviour	
	Factor A 1 Pressing for change	Factor A 2 Questioning authority	Factor B 1 Pressing for change	Factor B 2 Questioning authority
	(weighting given)			
1 Cautious/audacious	15	64	72	21
2 Complying/questioning	37	35	67	29
3 Changing things/leaving well enough alone	72	(2·0) —03	74	10
4 Rule-abiding/rule evading	—01	72	02	80
5 Accepting authority/questioning authority	12	68	17	81
6 Imaginative/down-to-earth	48	(1·0) 19	71	10
7 Argumentative/acquiescent	71	(2·0) 15	51	47
8 Changing/stable	55	(1·0) 15	62	31
9 Rebelling/conforming	42	58	52	60
10 Using tried ideas/trying new ideas	58	(1·0) 21	77	00
11 Taking chances/playing safe	31	59	72	28
Percentage of total variance	31·3	11·1	45·3	11·8
Mean intercorrelations between items marked	r = 0·26	r = 0·38	r = 0·46	r = 0·44

Note: decimal points omitted.

factor analysis of data from Pugh et al. (1968) which cannot be identically reproduced with the present data. It is necessary therefore to return to the full primary measures of structure first used by Pugh and his colleagues. A close examination of the calculations employed by Inkson et al. on their pilot questionnaire data, including their factor analysis, made it clear also that the new data would not support an exact repetition of the measures (item combinations) which they used for role routine and definition or for the scoring of nonconforming behaviour. The measures of role formalization and conflict are, however, exactly the same as Inkson's. It should also be noted that in both studies the level of intercorrelation between items incorporated into composite measures tended to be low, although the samples of respondents in the two studies were large by most standards. The calculations leading to the formulation of measures were performed on the individual returns from the sample of managers; individual scores were subsequently computed for each manager and only after this stage were organizational means calculated.

Results

The purpose of this article is to explore relationships between variables located at different levels of organizational analysis, using the model of administrative reduction of variance in behaviour as a framework. A complete test of the model itself cannot be provided since the main procedure followed, the use of correlational analysis on cross-sectional data, does not allow for the necessary imputation of causality. A limited evaluation of the model is, however, possible given the apparently slow rate of change in the structures of British work organizations (Inkson et al., 1970, p. 322). For this reduces the likelihood that differential time-lags between changes in variables will produce misleading correlations. Correlations of close to zero obtained with cross-sectional data would in this instance probably constitute grounds for rejecting causal connections suggested by the model, as would correlations in the reverse direction to those predicted. All the correlation coefficients quoted in the text from this point on refer to the sample of seventy-eight organizations.

The correlations obtained between variables of organization context and structure are given in Table 3.4. These are in the main similar to the results obtained from previous studies employing the same or comparable measures. They illustrate the rationale behind the left-hand side of Figure 3.1.

Table 3.4
Product–moment correlations between selected variables of organization structure and context N = 78 organizations

Organization context variables	Organization structure variables					
	Functional speciali-zation	Role speciali-zation	Standardi-zation	Formali-zation	Recording of role performance	Centrali-zation
Size of organization: log of numbers employed	63***	66***	62***	58***	32**	—56***
Size of parent organization: log of numbers employed	54***	53***	61***	57***	43***	—32**
Workflow integration	41***	37***	26*	09	25*	14
Concentration of ownership (N = 46 only)	—15	—11	—29	—43**	—17	47***

Note: decimal points omitted
*p < ·15
**p < ·01
***p < ·001

32

Size of organization and size of parent organization are both positively related to the structuring variables of specialization, standardization and formalization. Size of organization is negatively related to centralization of decision making. Workflow integration is moderately related in a positive direction to specialization, standardization and recording of role performance. Another study using the same data, however, has indicated that when organization size is partialled out the strength of these relationships is decreased, but a positive relationship of workflow integration to centralization emerges (Child and Mansfield, 1972). Concentration of ownership with control is positively related to centralization. It is negatively related with formalization and, more weakly, with standardization.

Table 3.5

Product-moment correlations between organizational and managerial work role variables N = 78 organizations

Organizational variables	Managerial work role variables					
	Formali-zation	Defi-nition	Routine: problems and skills	Every-day routine	Long-term stability	Perceived authority
Context:						
Size of organization	24*	05	—22	—38***	—20	29**
Size of parent organization	59***	16	—15	—25*	—20	22
Workflow integration	04	26*	17	15	—10	—39***
Concentration of ownership (N = 46 only)	—28	24	06	21	—06	—32*
Structure:						
Functional specialization	48***	27*	—11	—21	—25*	07
Role specialization	52***	35**	—04	—22	—28*	14
Standardization	68***	28*	—20	—21	—27*	24*
Formalization	64***	14	—25*	—22	—24*	27*
Recording of role performance	59***	29**	—05	02	—21	11
Centralization	—31**	08	45***	51***	32**	—57***

Note: decimal points omitted

*p < ·05

**p < ·01

***p < ·001

The argument centring on specificity of role prescription expressed in Figure 3.1 postulates that the structuring variables – and to a lesser extent their contextual precursors – will be positively related to role formalization, definition and routine. Equally, centralization of decision making is hypothesized to be negatively related to levels of perceived authority. Inkson et al. also suggested that there would be a general tendency for centralization and other aspects of role prescription to be positively related. The results presented in Table 3.5 indicate that, for senior managers at least, the pattern of relationships between organizational and role variables is somewhat more complex than the model suggests. The hypothesized positive relationship of structuring (specialization, standardization and formalization) to role formalization and role definition is supported. The hypothesis, however, is not supported for the three variables of role routine. The relationships between structuring and routine variables are consistently negative, though they are always low in value. There is also a general tendency for larger size of organization to be associated with a lower level of perceived routine in senior managerial roles and this association is strongest in relation to everyday routine.

This set of findings is similar to the results obtained by Inkson et al. (Table 2.1) except that they reported a stronger negative association between routine and the structuring variables. The different directions in which role definition and role routine are each related to organizational variables also suggest that specificity of role prescription as formulated by Hickson (see Chapter 1) is not a unitary concept. In fact, the maximum variance shared between role definition and a role routine variable is 12 per cent, where $r = 0.34$ between definition and routine in respect to problems and skills. Similarly, while role formalization is related to role definition ($r = 0.49$), it is not related to variables of routine.

The negative correlation shown in Table 3.5 between centralization of decision making and the perceived level of managerial authority ($r = -0.57$) becomes more understandable when it is explained that a high score on the measure of centralization which was used would typically signify that many decisions were being confined to the chief executive level or were even being taken outside the organization altogether by an owning group or by a nonexecutive board. At the same time centralization emerges as a predictor of routine among managers, especially concerning their everyday schedule of activities and concerning the intrinsic nature of problems to be dealt with. When decision making in organizations is more centralized, managers appear to be left with a greater share of routine activities. At the same time Table 3.5 also suggests that in these circumstances managers' responsibilities tend to be less well prescribed in official documents such as job descriptions (role formalization).

The relationship of perceived authority to other variables is, with one exception, reasonably predictable from a knowledge of the above results. The exception lies in the finding that managers in organizations with a higher degree of technological integration (workflow integration) tend to see themselves as enjoying lower levels of authority ($r = -0.39$). This particular relationship is in fact strengthened when the effects of organization size are partialled out (partial $r = -0.49$). It would seem that more integrated and less variable workflows provide a more placid and less uncertain organizational environment in which there is less evidence of pressures to delegate authority in order to ensure a rapid response to changing circumstances. As the model would lead one to expect, organization size is found to be positively related with the perceived level of managerial authority, while concentration of ownership is negatively related to the measure of role routine: to routine in problems and skills ($r = -0.40$), to everyday routine ($r = -0.49$), and to long-term job stability ($r = -0.24$).

The administrative reduction of variance thesis also postulates that, because of their supposed effects on role variables, both the structuring of activities and centralization will be conducive to relatively cautious and conformist behaviour and to a reduction in the degree of conflict. This hypothesis suggests an examination of results in terms of the links which are projected first to the degree on nonconforming behaviour and second to the level of conflict. Relevant data are provided in Table 3.6.

The administrative reduction of variance model leads one to expect that a greater structuring of activities within organizations will be negatively associated with nonconformity in behaviour. The data in Table 3.6 indicate that managers' expectations about an appropriate degree of nonconformity, in the form of questioning authority or pressing for change, were not predicted by the level of structuring (specialization, standardization). Nor does it appear that the structuring of activities is predictive of the degree of nonconforming behaviour that is actually perceived as taking place. The structuring of activities is, however, also associated with size of organization. When partial correlations are performed controlling for size of organization, a positive relationship appears between the extent to which formal authority is seen to be challenged and the level of standardization (partial $r = 0.40$) and the level of formalization (partial $r = 0.33$). This finding would be consistent with the view that the more bureaucratic formality in an organization of a given size, the more managers are led to challenge its relevance. The absence of many strong links between the structuring of activities and

Table 3.6
Product-moment correlations between organizational, managerial work role and behavioural variables N = 78 organizations

Organizational variables	Behavioural variables				
	Expected behaviour		Perceived behaviour		
	Questioning authority	Pressing for change	Questioning authority	Pressing for change	Conflict
Context:					
Size of organization	16	25*	—14	—01	—05
Size of parent organization	10	17	09	07	11
Workflow integration	—26*	—03	—21	—21	06
Concentration of ownership (N = 46 only)	—14	—31*	18	15	01
Structure:					
Functional specialization	—04	07	07	—05	33**
Role specialization	07	10	08	00	23*
Standardization	15	18	22	06	31**
Formalization	17	18	19	10	27*
Recording of role performance	—01	—01	17	12	44***
Centralization	—46***	—39***	—19	—21	—01
Work role variables:					
Formalization	08	19	33**	08	36**
Definition	—27*	—15	06	02	08
Routine: problems and skills	—48***	—44***	—37***	—38***	—03
Everyday routine	—34***	—35**	—22	—34**	13
Long-term stability	—33**	—28*	—21	—17	—20
Perceived authority	46***	31	43***	27*	—03

Note: decimal points omitted.
*p < ·05
**p < ·01
***p < ·001

nonconformity contrasts with the finding reported by Inkson et al. in Chapter 2 that structuring of activities had a quite high positive association with their measure of expected nonconforming behaviour, which incorporated both the questioning authority and pressing for change type of items.

Centralization of decision making emerges as a much stronger predictor of managerial expectations about. questioning authority and about pressing for change. The more centralized the overall level of decision making within an organization the less managers regard questioning authority and pressing for change as appropriate modes of behaviour. There is also in centralized organizations a tendency for behavioural patterns actually perceived at the managerial level to be more cautious and conforming. This association strengthens somewhat when size of organization is controlled: the partial r between centralization and perceived levels of questioning authority is —0·33, while that between centralization and perceived levels of pressing for change is —0·26.

The data suggest the presence of two mediating variables between the centralization of decision making and the lack of nonconforming behaviour. Centralized organization structures are found to be associated with managers perceiving their authority to be relatively low and their role routine relatively high. Low authority and high routine are in turn both associated with highly conforming behaviour as can be seen from the lower portion of Table 3.6. This is the kind of situation in which path analysis can make a useful contribution in distinguishing the weight which should be given to direct and indirect relationships. The problem is that path analysis requires an assumption that there is an asymmetrical causal chain, in this case from the organization level variable (overall centralization) through the role level variables (authority and routine) to the behavioural variable (conformity). This is precisely the assumption underlying the model of administrative reduction of variance in behaviour, but an assumption we are not able to test with the data available. It was felt, however, that, while the use of path analysis cannot be demonstrated as completely justified, it would none the less be suggestive to use it in an examination of the links between centralization and behaviour, accepting for the moment that the causal assumptions in the administrative reduction of variance model are valid. Path analysis was therefore applied to the association between centralization of decision making and the level of questioning authority seen as appropriate by managers, selected because it enjoyed the highest zero-order correlation with centralization. The results of the analysis, shown in Figure 3.2, do turn out to be of interest. For they suggest that virtually the whole 'effect' of centralized decision making on the behavioural level variable is indirect, through its prior 'effects' on the levels of role routine and authority. This type of finding would, of course, be consistent with the administrative reduction of variance model in which the effects of structural variables are postulated to operate on behaviour primarily through role prescription. But it cannot, we repeat, be regarded as a test of whether the model's causal assumptions are valid.

Turning to the level of conflict between managers, the relationships suggested by the administrative reduction of variance model are not found

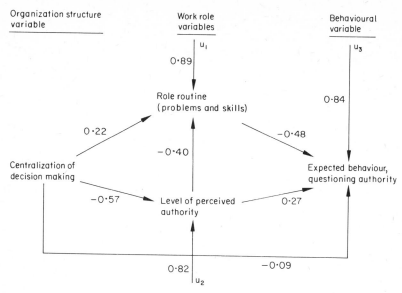

Figure 3.2   Relationships between centralization and expected level of
questioning authority

in the data. The consistent tendency, shown in Table 3.6, for all the
structuring of activities variables to relate positively with the level of
conflict is the reverse of the model's predictions. Two broad explanations
are possible. The attempt to structure activities in designing organizations
could be a response to high levels of conflict; that is, it could represent an
attempt to control and regulate the situation. This is a reverse causal
sequence to that postulated by the model. Alternatively, the structural
features could be acting in unintended and unanticipated ways to
encourage conflict. Students of bureaucracy have provided empirical
documentation of such unanticipated consequences, though at lower
levels in the hierarchy (March and Simon, 1958).

    The strongest relationships found were between the level of conflict and
recording of role performance, functional specialization, and standardization, respectively. These correlations all rise when the effects of
organization size are removed. In other words, there tends to be greater
conflict among the managers of departments (1) the more specialized
departments an organization has, (2) the more it relies upon standard
rules and procedures which in many cases will be applied by one
department to the operations of other departments and (3) the more role
performance is recorded on paper (again usually involving the monitoring
by one area of others). Expressed in these terms as an effect of structure

upon behaviour, the results obtained have considerable face validity. Whatever their explanation they do not however, conform to the administrative reduction of variance thesis, nor do the correlations obtained between work role variables and the level of conflict.

With the same qualifications as were previously expressed, the application of path analysis may again be employed to explore the direct and indirect links between organizational variables and the levels of conflict between managers. In Figure 3.3 we have chosen to compare the direct links between standardization and conflict and between recording of role performance and conflict, with their indirect links through the level of role formalization. In the case of standardization the picture which emerges is not apparent from a simple inspection of the zero-order correlations. The overall zero-order correlation between standardization of procedures and conflict is $r = 0.31$. The path analysis gives a negative path coefficient for the direct relationship between the two variables of —0·29, but also indicates that there is a positive relationship through role formalization and the recording of role performance.

These results suggest that (1) in so far as the use of standard

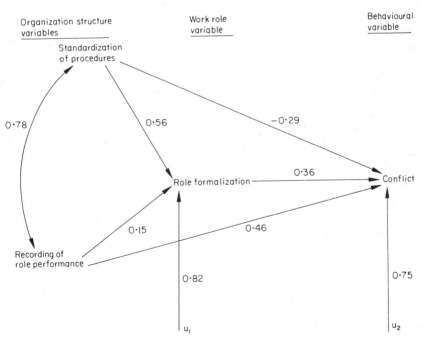

Fig. 3.3 Relationships between standardization, recording of role performance and interpersonal conflict

procedures (or at least some types of procedures) provides points of reference which permit the prescription of managerial roles in official documents, standardization promotes conflict between managers. On the other hand, (2) the use of standard procedures *per se* (or at least of other types of procedure) reduces the level of such conflict. The direct negative link between standardization and conflict possibly reflects the fact that many procedures are in effect designed to remove sources of disagreement by stipulating what shall be done, who shall be involved, and the like. To the extent that a highly standardized system also facilitates the documentation of managerial roles themselves and of departmental performance, however, the result appears to be a higher level of conflict between managers. When functional specialization is substituted for standardization in the analysis, a similar result emerges, with positive indirect links to conflict through the level of role formalization and through the recording of role performance. The direct link in this case is essentially nil, a path coefficient of —0·01.

While the direct link between standardization and conflict is a negative one, that between recording of role performance and conflict is a positive one. The indirect link from recording of role performance through role formalization to conflict emerges as almost nonexistent, and the analysis suggests that it is the use of performance-orientated records themselves which is a source of conflict. The path analysis suggests these conclusions, but they clearly require further examination using longitudinal or processual data.

Centralization of decision making and the level of perceived authority have no apparent association with the level of conflict. The present results do not confirm Inkson et al.'s finding in Chapter 2 of a negative relationship between centralization and the level of conflict. On the other hand it may also be noted that the relationships found between conflict and the structuring of activities were not evident in the Inkson study.

A higher level of conflict tended to be accompanied by a greater perceived level of questioning authority among managers ($r = 0.37$), but —0·20). It may be that difficulty in reaching agreement among themselves is one factor in managers' perceptions which differentiates between the two one factor in managers' perceptions which differentiates between the two aspects of nonconforming behaviour measured. There are two causal possibilities here. Questioning formal authority and rules possibly breeds conflict, while pursuing new ideas does not necessarily do so. To reverse the causality, the presence of disagreement between managers may encourage the challenging of authority but, if anything, it may inhibit the pursuit of innovation.

40

Finally, the correlations between variables of organization context and those of managerial behaviour are generally weak (Table 3.6). They tend to be even weaker than the correlations between contextual variables and work role variables, and this progressive weakening of relationships is consistent with the administrative reduction of variance model.

Conclusion

The data reported were located within a model of the administrative reduction of variance in behaviour, described in Figure 3.1. They allowed for a limited evaluation to be made of the model. Its pivotal concept, Hickson's specificity of role prescription, proved to be multidimensional. The degree of role routine perceived by managers was distinct from their perceived level of role definition, and distinct from the formalization of their roles. Higher levels of role routine were positively associated with centralized decision making. The chain of relationships posited by the model to run from centralization through specificity of role prescription to conformity of behaviour was not refuted by the data, although no relationship appeared between centralization and levels of conflict. The relationships posited between the structuring of activities and role variables were tentatively supported for role formalization and definition, but not for role routine. Links between structuring of activities and the degree of nonconforming behaviour were only observed with the perceived degree of questioning authority, and even then they were the reverse of what the model hypothesized. The positive relationship found between the structuring of activities variables and conflict – mediated, it appears, by the level of role formalization – was also the reverse of that originally expected. In general, the relationships which emerged between the variables located at different levels of organizational analysis are more complex than had been envisaged in Inkson et al.'s exposition of the administrative reduction of variance model in Chapter 2.

The findings reported here lend some support to the view that a more accurate understanding of behaviour in organizations can be obtained if the organizational environment of that behaviour is precisely described. Thus, in the present investigation a more centralized pattern of decision making – implying that many decisions are confined to chief executive level or above – emerges as a major potential source of routine in managers' activities and ultimately of conformist attitudes regarding appropriate behaviour. The word potential is used advisedly because causality cannot be demonstrated. The manner in which structural, role, and behavioural characteristics are associated is, however, complex and is likely to be contingent upon the people involved, their place in the organization, and other features of the particular situation. For example the bureaucratic properties incorporated in the structuring variables unexpectedly do not appear to possess a potential for reducing behavioural variance among senior managers. If anything, the reverse may be true, a conclusion reached both in this study and by Inkson et al. (1968).

One likely reason is that senior managers tend to be located above the organizational levels to which most bureaucratic controls are directed. Also, in so far as a system of controls does constrain the operation of their departments and does define their own roles, senior managers are normally in a position to challenge that system openly and in so doing will probably be drawn into conflict with their colleagues. Quite different results might have emerged if we had studied a sample of lower level personnel, possibly indicating, as Argyris (1957) has argued, that for such employees specialization, standardization and formalization do induce conformity and do constrain conflict.

Centralized decision making was found to be linked through perceived authority and role routine to expectations of conforming behaviour, but not to levels of conflict. Structuring of activities variables were linked directly or indirectly to levels of conflict, but not in the main to conforming behaviour. These two sets of findings suggest that the personal consequences of control strategies for managers are different. The centralization of decision making implies a personal mode of control, which tends to be found in smaller organizations having closer links with ownership (see Table 3.4). It is understandable that in such situations manager's should expect conformity and caution to be appropriate modes of behaviour. The exercise of administrative control indirectly and impersonally through bureaucratic mechanisms, however, places managers in a different personal position. They will now be the makers as well as the recipients of decisions on specialization and on procedural and paperwork systems. While a bureaucratic structure may add some definition to their duties and formal authority, it does not add to their own degree of role routine. An ostensible purpose of the structure is, in fact, to permit senior managers to give more time to nonroutine issues by delegating some routinized work. The accentuation of departmentalization and of interdepartmental controls which is also implied in the bureaucratic approach increases the difficulty of reaching agreements on issues which arise for collective managerial discussion.

Speculations such as these require further empirical testing using methods very different from the cross-sectional approach employed in this article. They bear upon problems of some moment for those concerned with organizational development, and in this respect the findings can serve to offer one important guideline. For if it is the case that organizational variables are relevant to an understanding of behaviour, even at senior managerial level, an attempt to modify such behaviour merely by adjusting individual characteristics as the result of training will probably be inadequate and potentially stressful for the manager when returning to his unchanged organizational environment. Organizational modifications are also required, a fact which is becoming increasingly appreciated today by practitioners in the field of planned change.

4 Placing stereotypes of the manager into perspective*

TONY ELLIS and JOHN CHILD

Introduction

Management selection relies in principle upon the development of criteria for effective performance in the job and upon the identification of personal characteristics which are presumed to be good predictors of that performance. Such considerations form the basis for expectations as to the appropriate outlook and style of behaviour in particular managerial jobs. These expectations both reflect and reinforce stereotypes of managers that are related to factors such as the type of organization, the industry or the functional area in which jobs are located. The wide currency of stereotypes is not, however, a sign that we possess well-established information about different groups of managers. On the contrary, managerial stereotypes have only infrequently been subject to systematic investigation.

One of the more broadly-defined, yet popular and influential, images of modern managers is that of 'bureaucratic man' or its close relative 'organization man'. Here, the routine, formality and rationality of contemporary large-scale organization is seen to impose rigid, cautious and compliant behaviour as a norm of acceptability among the members. Merton's (1940) classic analysis of 'bureaucratic structure and personality' developed this stereotype, while Whyte (1960) had a large hand in popularizing it. Other popular stereotypes which refer to particular organizational contexts include industry-based images such as the 'advertising man' described by Tunstall (1964) or banking employment as analysed by McMurry (1958). Then there are occupationally or functionally based stereotypes such as those attached to 'marketing men', 'research men', or 'finance men' within management. Burns and Stalker (1961) have, for example, described some of the problems of collaboration which can accompany the distinctive orientations and

* originally published in *Journal of Management Studies,* vol. 10, 1973, pp. 233–55.

modes of behaviour of research personnel in organizations. There are also cultural based stereotypes which have been applied to managers. These underlie the largely impressionistic discussions of differences between British and American 'philosophies of management' (e.g. Mace, 1952; Dubin, 1970).

All these stereotypes contain implicit hypotheses that managers differ significantly in terms of their working and social contexts. These hypotheses are worthy of testing, especially as in the case of bureaucratic man some evidence already suggests that the stereotype is misleading. Blau (1955) found, for example, that, contrary to the stereotype, the employees of a government bureaucracy held favourable attitudes towards change, largely because of the job security which the organization provided. Similarly, Kohn (1971) found that men working in bureaucracies tended to be intellectually more flexible, more receptive to new experience and more self-directed in their values than those employed in nonbureaucratic organizations. Again, these characteristics appeared in part to be shared by people who had been attracted to bureaucratic employment because of its advantageous working conditions. The question is therefore raised as to what extent characteristics of bureaucratic employees are associated with the presence of bureaucracy per se compared with other concomitants of large-scale organization such as higher pay, greater job security and more extended career ladders. An individual's hierarchical position may also mediate the possibly constrictive socio-psychological consequences of bureaucratic structure. Argyris (1957) has argued that senior personnel do not feel the effects of structural controls on behaviour as much as lower-level employees. Vroom (1964) cites findings which tend to support this assertion, namely that higher levels of management are more likely to be concerned with personal growth, self-actualization and autonomy than are people further down the hierarchy.

Reference to bureaucratic man, as well as to the supposed conservatism of British management when compared with American, has frequently been in the context of examining the conditions for greater effectiveness and faster economic growth. Performance in managerial jobs is assumed to have a particularly direct bearing on the success of an organization as a whole. However, many of the available research studies of managers have concentrated on their satisfaction with the immediate work environment rather than on their general orientations towards change or towards other factors which might be more directly associated with the level of performance achieved by their organizations (cf. the reviews of studies compiled by Porter and Lawler, 1965; Cummings and El Salmi, 1968).

Pym's (1966) work on the characteristics of managers who are able to perform effectively in conditions of change remains fairly exceptional.

These considerations form the background to the present report on 787 senior managers employed in 78 British companies. Among the data collected were brief biographical details of each manager, information on his formal qualifications, indications of his personal flexibility in the work context and data on his normative attitudes to behaviour at his level of the organization. These data and their relation to structural, contextual and performance variables are reported in this paper.

Sample and procedure

The data reported here were collected as part of a broader study into the possible relationships between role, organizational and performance variables within contrasting environments. A sample of organizations was therefore drawn from six British *industries* with the intention of obtaining a contrast in terms of two major criteria: (1) the manufacturing-service dichotomy and (2) variability *versus* relative stability in product and technological environments. The six industries can be located

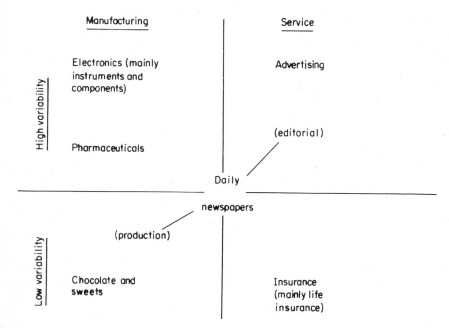

Fig. 4.1   Industries in the sample

46

approximately in the following paradigm, bearing in mind that some industries (such as electronics) are fairly heterogeneous in terms of the environments in which their organizations are operating. Two industries were selected for the high variability/manufacturing category because this was the area upon which many previous organizational studies had concentrated (see Figure 4.1).

Daily newspaper organizations represent a 'hybrid' case in this paradigm. They contain an important service element (editorial) as well as a manufacturing one (production). The parameters of editorial work content are subject to a high degree of variability, while those of production are not.

Within the six industries, 82 organizations were studied for the research programme, data being collected from late 1967 to the end of 1969. Chief executives in 78 of these companies gave permission for the despatch of a questionnaire to their managers, and these 78 constitute the sample of organizations which will be referred to in this chapter. The intention was to select organizations which would cluster as closely as possible around certain *size levels* in terms of total numbers employed – 150, 300, 500, 1,000, 2,500 and 5,000 persons. In practice this proved difficult to achieve with the higher size levels. The object of this stratification was to obtain contrasts in organizational size within the sample as a whole while retaining a consistency of size levels across organizations in the different industries. The attention given to size at the sampling stage was prompted by the important predictive role played by this variable in previous organizational research (cf. Pugh et al., 1969).

The mean organizational size and standard deviations actually achieved for each level, together with the distribution by industry, are shown in Table 4.1. The main peculiarity in this distribution is the absence of any advertising organizations at the two highest size levels, because none existed in Britain at the time of the study. Figures for each organization's size are not shown in order to avoid identification.

In each organization a comprehensive measure was attempted along the primary dimensions of *organizational structure* operationalized by Pugh et al. (1968). Data on organizational structure were collected by means of interviews with departmental managers in each company. Four dimensions of structure were included in this particular analysis:

Specialization: (1) Functional specialization – the extent to which official duties are divided between discrete identifiable functional areas.

                (2) Role specialization – the extent to which official duties are divided within functional areas between

	discrete identifiable positions.
Standardization:	The extent to which activities are subject to standard procedure and rules.
Formalization:	The extent to which procedures, rules, instructions and communications are written down.
Centralization:	The extent to which the locus of authority to make decisions affecting the organization is confined to the higher levels of the hierarchy.

A conjunction of specialization, standardization, formalization and decentralization constitutes the main elements of bureaucratic structure as described by Weber (1947) and many others.

In three of the selected industries – advertising, electronics and pharmaceuticals – some of the companies studied were American-owned. The contrast between *American and British ownership* of companies located in Britain makes it possible to examine whether there are different types of managers and management philosophies in the two categories of company. The distribution of organizations by industry and ownership is:

	Number of organizations	
Industry	British-owned	American-owned
Advertising	5	7
Electronics*	11	5
Pharmaceuticals*	8	2

*Also 1 company owned on continental Europe.

Data on managerial level variables were collected by means of a postal questionnaire from senior managers in the 78 companies which have been described. For this managerial sample, heads of departments in 13 specified functional areas were selected from each organization, together with any other managers (but not assistants) reporting directly to the chief executive. In some organizations the full range of functional managers was not present. In certain other organizations there were several heads of department falling within a single function, such as several divisional production managers. The response rate for the questionnaire sent to these managers, between one and two weeks after completing the investigation of organizational variables, was 88·6 per cent. This response provided 787 usable returns.

The *functions* from which managers were chosen are listed below, along with the number of respondents in each one. Workflow (production)

Table 4.1
Sample of organization studied

Size level (employees)	Industry					
	Manufacturing				Service	
	Chocolate and sweets	Electronics	Daily newspapers	Pharma-ceuticals	Advertising	Insurance
mean:153·5 s.d. : 25·0	**	***	*	*	***	**
mean:313·1 s.d. : 42·4	**	***	**	***	***	**
mean:500·8 s.d. : 42·0	*	***	***	**	****	**
mean:1212·8 s.d. : 280·2	**	**	****	**	**	***
mean:2338·6 s.d. : 273·5	*	***	**	**	—	**
mean:6347·5 s.d. :1763·4	*	***	***	*	—	***

* = one company studied; total number = 78.

control, maintenance and work study have been combined into a 'Workflow ancillary' category, while Transport and a few other managers (mainly EDP) have been categorized as 'Miscellaneous':

		N
1	Workflow (production or equivalent)	228
2	Marketing/customer contact	178
3	Finance	89
4	Personnel	65
5	Design/research	54
6	Administration (*e.g.* company secretary)	46
7	Workflow ancillary	44
8	Buying	33
9	Quality control/inspection	25
10	Miscellaneous	25
	Total	$N = 787$

If a manager was responsible for more than one of these functional areas, he was classified under the function which on investigation was found to occupy most of his time and resources.

The three sampling parameters just described – industry, organizational size and managerial function – together with company ownership and organizational structure, allow us to examine managerial characteristics in relation to their context on a comparative basis. Before presenting the results of this examination, a description of how managerial characteristics were measured is also required.

Measurement of managerial characteristics

The questionnaire asked about five features of the manager's personal background: his age, how long he had been employed in his present organization, how many different positions he had held, how long he had held his present position, and his formal qualifications. The data on qualifications were scored in the following manner which attempts to provide a scale of 'level of qualifications':

Level of qualification	score
(a) Higher degree (exclude Oxbridge and Scottish MA)	8
(b) University degree, plus professional qualification (A), plus other examinable qualification (B)	7
(c) University degree, plus professional qualification (A) only	6
(d) University degree, plus other examinable qualification (B) only	5
(e) University degree only	4
(f) Professional qualification (A), plus other examinable qualification (B)	3
(g) Professional qualification (A) only	2
(h) Other examinable qualification (B) only	1
(i) No recognized qualification	0

The term 'university degree' refers to undergraduate degrees. Professional qualifications (A) were those appearing in Millerson's list (1964, Appendix I) (A) of qualifying associations holding their own examination. An example is the Institute of Chartered Accountants. Other examinable qualifications (B) referred to grades of membership or qualifications of associations in Millerson's list (B): associations not holding their own examinations but using evidence of external examinations, for example, the Institution of Plant Engineers. This category was also taken to include National Diploma or Certificate qualifications (ONC, OND, HNC,

Table 4.2
Personal flexibility: principal components analysis (varimax rotation)
N = 787

Items (abbreviated from questionnaire and in re-arranged order)	Factor I 'Preference for a varied work environment'	Factor II 'Risk-taking'
1 dislikes a regular pattern	0·70	0·07
2 enjoys new, unusual circumstances	0·64	0·15
3 likes uncertainty in work	0·61	0·35
4 prefers job which is always changing	0·59	0·27
5 doesn't dislike having to change plans	0·57	—0·08
6 doesn't mind doing more than one thing at a time	0·42	—0·30
7 likes taking risks	0·18	0·73
8 has done dangerous things for a thrill	0·09	0·72
9 doesn't believe in one best way to solve problems	0·12	—0·01
10 changes mind often	—0·01	0·22
Percentage of total variance accounted for	26·0%	11·8%
Mean intercorrelation between items marked, which were used for constructing measures	0·30	0·31

HND). If a manager held more than one professional qualification (A), then he was scored 7 (if he had a degree) or 3 (if he had no degree).

A measure of personal flexibility in the work context was included in the questionnaire, and this represented a further development of the measure used by Pym (1966) in his studies of characteristics of the 'versatile' employee. A summary of the ten items employed is given in Table 4.2 which also records the main results from subjecting the data obtained to a principal components analysis. This analysis suggested the presence of several underlying dimensions to the data, the major one appearing to concern the manager's 'preference for a varied work environment'. Pym reports that for a sample of 548 mechanical engineers the correlations between his six items ranged from 0·28 to 0·05. This suggests the presence of multi-dimensionality among the items, but Pym does not appear to have examined this possibility further. Correlations between our ten items ranged from 0·36 to 0·00 for the 787 respondents, and several dimensions are clearly present within the original concept of flexibility in the work context. Scores were computed of 'preference for a varied work environment' and for 'risk-taking' by summing scores on the items marked under the two headings in Table 4.2.

A similar procedure was adopted with a set of eleven 7-point semantic differential items which respondents had been asked to score in regard to how they felt managers at, or about, their own level *ought* ideally to behave in carrying out their own jobs. The items had all been included in the questionnaire as potential measures of the extent to which managers were normatively inclined to favour innovative behaviour. However, the results of a principal components analysis, shown in Table 4.3, suggested some differentiation between items which refer primarily to the questioning of formal authority and rules, and items which provide a more general description of 'pressing for change'. The item intercorrelations for this measure were generally very low (mean r for all 11 items = 0·24) and it must be regarded as a candidate for further development (correlations between the same items incorporated in a subsequent question on how managers perceived actual behaviour were, however, much higher). The items marked in Table 4.3 were used to construct two

Table 4.3
Expected managerial behaviour: principal components analysis (varimax rotation) N = 787

Items (order as in questionnaire)	Expected behaviour		Factor II 'Questioning authority'
	Factor I 'Pressing for change' (weighting given)		
1 cautious/audacious	0·15		0·64
2 complying/questioning	0·37		0·35
3 changing things/leaving well alone	0·72|	(2·0)	0·03
4 rule-abiding/rule evading	—0·01		0·72|
5 accepting authority/questioning authority	0·12		0·68|
6 imaginative/down-to-earth	0·48|	(1·0)	0·19
7 argumentative/acquiescent	0·71|	(2·0)	0·15
8 changing/stable	0·55|	(1·0)	0·15
9 rebelling/conforming	0·42		0·58|
10 using tried ideas/trying new ideas	0·58|	(1·0)	0·21
11 taking chances/playing safe	0·31		0·59
Percentage of total variance	31·3%		11·1%
Mean intercorrelations between items marked	$r = 0·26$		$r = 0·38$

measures: (1) five items were given the weightings shown and then summed to form a measure of expected 'pressing for change'; (2) three items were summed to form a measure of expected 'questioning authority'. These latter three items were selected so as to be directly comparable with a measure of perceived 'questioning authority' described elsewhere (Child and Ellis, 1973).

Finally, it should be noted that, in reporting associations between personal managerial characteristics and organizational variables such as structure and company performance, the individual scores for the managers in each organization have been averaged. Although Guilford (1956) has pointed to problems with aggregating individual scores in this way, the nature of our sampling and the high response rate do permit the suggestion that the aggregations in this case are reasonably acceptable as characterizations of the senior management in the organization as a whole.

In search of bureaucratic man

Specialization, standardization and formalization are highly related features of organization structure (mean $r = 0·77$) and they are moderately related negatively with centralization of decision making (mean $r = —0·41$). High values on these variables (with low values on centralization) indicate that an organization is 'bureaucratic' in terms of Weber's classic definition, while a conjunction of high centralization and low levels of specialization, standardization and formalization would indicate a relatively 'nonbureaucratic' organizational setting (cf. Child, 1972a).

The results presented in Table 4.4 at first sight suggest that managers working within bureaucratic environments are, much as Kohn (1971) found, more flexible individuals. Their scores on 'preference for a varied work environment' are positively correlated with specialization, standardization and formalization and negatively correlated with centralization of decision making. Scores on 'risk-taking' are similarly associated with bureaucratization though rather weakly. Moreover, managers located within bureaucracies appear to have higher levels of qualification, to have held more different jobs and to have been in their present position for a shorter period of time. Thus it would seem that bureaucracies do not have bureaucrats working for them in terms of the commonly held stereotype, at least at their more senior levels.

However, we cannot conclude the matter at this point as there is a

Table 4.4
Product–moment correlations between features of bureaucratic organization, size of organization and managerial characteristics
N = 78 organizations[a]
(Correlations in parentheses are with size of organization partialled out)

Managerial variables (averaged by organization)	Functional speciali- zation	Role speciali- zation	Standardi- zation	Formali- zation	Centrali- zation	Size of organization (log. total employees)
Personal background						
1 Age	05	03	—05	—02	00	31[c]
	(—20)	(—25)	(—33)	(—25)	(22)	
2 Level of qualifications	24[b]	27[b]	33[c]	41[d]	—40[d]	29[c]
	(07)	(11)	(20)	(32)	(—30)	
3 Length of time in organization (years)	—09	—08	—10	—04	05	34[c]
	(—42)	(—44)	(—42)	(—30)	(31)	
4 Number of positions held	19	23[b]	24[b]	32[c]	—32[c]	59[d]
	(—29)	(—26)	(—20)	(—03)	(01)	
5 Time in present position	—29[b]	—27[b]	—28[b]	—24[b]	17	—18
	(—23)	(—21)	(—22)	(—17)	(08)	
Personal orientation						
6 Preference for varied work environment	37[d]	39[d]	43[d]	41[d]	—52[d]	49[d]
	(09)	(04)	(18)	(18)	(—34)	
7 Risk-taking	16	21	25[b]	24[b]	—32[c]	19
	(05)	(11)	(19)	(16)	(—27)	
8 Expectations on questioning authority	—04	07	15	17	—46[d]	16
	(—19)	(—04)	(07)	(09)	(—45)	
9 Expectations on pressing for change	07	10	18	18	—39[d]	25[b]
	(—12)	(—09)	(03)	(04)	(—31)	

[a] Decimal points omitted.
[b] $P < 0.05$
[c] $P < 0.01$
[d] $P < 0.001$

third factor in the situation which has a major influence. This is the size of the organization measured by total numbers employed. Larger organizations tend to be more specialized, to have more standard procedures and to rely more on paperwork (mean $r = 0.62$), and they also tend to be less centralized ($r = -0.56$). As Table 4.4 indicates, size is also associated with the presence of several personal characteristics among senior managers.

When the effects of size are eliminated statistically by partial correlation analysis, the association between organization structure and personal characteristics is modified. Bureaucracy now appears chiefly to be associated with a more youthful and qualified senior management, which on average has spent less time with the organization. Features of organization structure no longer predict managers' personal orientations, with the exception of centralization. The more highly centralized organizations have more rigid, conformist and conservatively-oriented senior managers than do others, and it may be noted that this conclusion holds true even when the (generally smaller) size of centralized organizations is taken into account.

In short, the data indicate that bureaucracies, contrary to the stereotype, tend to have younger, better qualified senior personnel who express more flexible and challenging attitudes; however, the presence of such attitudes is at least in part a function of the kind of people who seem to work in the upper echelons of *large* organizations, and who may have been attracted to such employment by the kind of associated benefits that Kohn has described. Implicit in the stereotype of bureaucratic man is the view that personal characteristics are moulded over time by bureaucratic structures, and less attention is paid to the self-selection of individuals with particular characteristics into bureaucracies. It is, however, possible to find evidence for both processes, and the presence of both would be quite compatible with our findings (cf. Schein, 1970).

In search of other managerial stereotypes

1 *Industry*

The personal backgrounds of senior managers in the six industries sampled vary considerably as is indicated by the analysis of variance given in Table 4.5. On most of the variables measured, the variance of scores within industries proved to be far less significant than the differences in industry means. This is not an altogether unexpected finding since the six industries had been selected to provide contrasting organizational environments.

Insurance managers emerge as a very distinctive category. Their average age is higher than that for other industries. Their average length of employment within their present organization far exceeds that for managers in the other industries; they have typically held almost two extra roles during that employment and the average length of time spent in their present role is also fairly high. Although it is today showing signs of

Table 4.5
Industry membership and managerial characteristics

Variable	Mean scores						F ratio	Level of confidence (P)
	Advertising N = 113	Insurance N = 133	Chocolate and sweets N = 75	Electronics N = 189	Newspapers N = 166	Pharmaceuticals N = 111		
Personal background								
1 Age	43·78	48·62	46·75	43·06	46·40	45·06	8·09	< 0·001
2 Level of qualifications	2·85	2·82	1·76	2·61	1·49	3·24	12·80	< 0·001
3 Length of time in organization (years)	12·44	25·11	15·85	10·71	16·18	14·14	30·28	< 0·001
4 Number of positions held	3·18	4·89	3·03	3·21	3·24	3·38	8·60	< 0·001
5 Time in present position	4·92	5·33	6·10	3·37	5·36	4·69	4·46	< 0·001
Personal orientation								
6 Preference for varied work environment	7.43	6·64	7·18	7·25	7·16	6·99	1·55	n.s.
7 Risk-taking	2·34	1·64	2·15	2·00	1·89	2·05	3·45	< 0·01
8 Expectations on questioning authority	15·89	12·55	11·46	13·19	13·45	13·25	7·44	< 0·001
9 Expectations on pressing for change	30·57	28·12	28·12	28·31	29·63	28·95	3·81	< 0·01

change, the career structure for insurance managers has traditionally been distinctive in the kind of respects our data have illustrated. At the other extreme, managers in electronics organizations had spent, on average, under half the average time for insurance managers with their present companies, and not much above half the average insurance time in their present positions. They were also, on average, five and a half years younger than insurance managers.

At a more general level of observation, the data on personal background suggest that organizations located in industries with a longer-established tradition, such as insurance, chocolate and sweets, and newspapers, tend to establish career patterns in which there is a norm of learning by 'experience' through a relatively long tenure of particular roles. In so far as this is the case, the learning of traditional methods will in these industries be given a heavy weighting along with (or even in contrast to) formal qualifications. It is apparent from Table 4.5 that managers in the chocolate/sweets and newspaper industries do in fact possess lower levels of qualification than is normal in the other industries.

The presence of statistically 'significant' discrimination between managers' personal orientations in terms of their industries is in large measure due to the particular distinctiveness of the 'advertising man'. He perceives himself as much more of a risk-taker than do other managers; he thinks that people at his level in the organization ought to question formal authority and press for change more than is the case with other managers. He also exhibits a greater preference for a varied environment, though overall this measure does not vary significantly according to the industry in which a manager works. The advertising manager thus emerges as very much an individualist, a conclusion which patterns of frequent job changing in the industry would seem to confirm. Insurance managers, as is popularly imagined, emerge as the least inclined to take risks in their personal conduct while, together with chocolate and sweet managers, they have the most conformist expectations regarding authority and change. These results do not hold any surprises, for in the main they lend support to the popular images which tend to be held of those working in the industries concerned.

2   Functional area

A similar conclusion emerges from Table 4.6 where a comparison is made between managers grouped according to their area of functional specialization. While there was no appreciable variation between the ages of managers according to their functional specialism, their career histories within their present organization did exhibit some differences. Thus managers of finance, buying and 'workflow ancillary' (production support) departments had experienced a relatively low rate of job rotation – they had generally held fewer different positions and had been incumbent in their present roles for a longer period than other managers. In contrast, managers in charge of design and research activities, personnel and marketing managers, tend to have experienced a higher rate of intra-organizational mobility. However, while design and personnel managers also had the highest average level of formal qualifications, marketing managers had the lowest.

The results on personal orientations indicate a clear and strong differentiation between design, personnel, marketing and workflow managers on the one hand, and other functional managers on the other. The former group exhibit high levels of personal flexibility in their attitudes towards variety in work environment and taking risks. A

Table 4.6
Functional specialism and managerial characteristics

Variable	Administration N = 46	Buying N = 33	Workflow ancillary N = 44	Design N = 54	Miscellaneous N = 25	Finance N = 89	Inspection N = 25	Marketing N = 178	Personnel N = 65	Workflow N = 228	F Ratio	Level of confidence (P)
Personal background												
1 Age	47·28	45·64	45·59	43·52	43·08	45·54	44·74	45·06	45·24	45·15	0·94	n.s.
2 Level of qualifications	2·51	2·17	2·08	4·35	2·52	2·38	2·84	1·92	3·08	2·33	6·88	< 0·001
3 Length of time in organization (years)	17·85	15·18	14·09	14·59	13·44	14·03	13·12	14·51	13·92	17·93	2·01	< 0·05
4 Number of positions held	3·67	2·42	3·00	3·73	2·88	2·84	3·10	3·55	3·33	4·06	2·75	< 0·01
5 Time in present position	4·48	6·91	4·72	3·52	4·48	6·52	4·64	4·32	4·00	5·27	2·48	< 0·01
Personal orientation												
6 Preference for varied work environment	7·13	7·00	6·81	7·98	6·44	5·82	6·52	7·31	7·26	7·42	4·62	< 0·001
7 Risk-taking	1·89	1·76	1·66	2·30	1·36	1·49	1·48	2·30	2·35	2·00	4·34	< 0·001
8 Expectations on questioning authority	11·65	12·40	11·93	13·79	10·36	11·55	10·60	14·38	14·32	14·37	5·66	< 0·001
9 Expectations on pressing for change	28·76	26·52	28·55	28·08	27·80	27·85	26·72	30·05	29·08	29·53	2·85	< 0·01

Mean scores by functional specialism

similar pattern of results also emerges in regard to expectations of behaviour, where differences are particularly marked concerning the challenging of formal authority and procedure. In contrast to the design, personnel, marketing and workflow group, financial managers and quality control managers emerge as the least flexible groups, and also the most conservative in regard to authority and innovation.

These fairly systematic differences in attitudes between functional groups within management may reflect not only the influence of prior occupational selection, socialization and a continued contact with external reference groups, but also the consequences of the different roles performed by such groups within the operating systems of their organizations. For the managers who exhibited more rigid and conservative attitudes were placed in a predominantly monitoring and 'controlling' role, while the contrasting groups generally comprised managers who had an important 'initiating' function within the organization.

The drawing of managerial stereotypes on the basis of differences in industry and functional specialism thus appears to gain a good deal of support from our research data. The way in which senior managers are distributed across different specialized functions is not, however, the same for firms located in different industries, either in the real world or in our sample, which tries to reflect it. For example, there are normally more senior design managers in electronics companies than in, say, chocolate and sweet companies. It is quite possible therefore that the findings described so far may reflect some interaction between the effect of a manager being in a particular industry and the effect of his being in charge of a particular functional area. We tested for this possibility using two-way analysis of variance. It did indeed emerge that the apparent industry effects on managers' scores for risk-taking and expected pressure for change were due primarily to the fact that functional area effects were not distributed equally among the six industries. This further analysis suggests the functional stereotypes provide better guidelines to managers' attitudes than do industry stereotypes, except with more extreme cases such as advertising managers. Within any one industry, managers' attitudes will vary considerably according to their functional area in the ways previously described.

3   Country of ownership

A great deal has been written on the supposed differences between the American and British, or European, 'philosophies of management'. In particular, a number of observers have concluded that British managerial attitudes and behaviour reflect an attachment to traditional values such as stability and conventionality which is not found amongst most American managers or among those working for American controlled companies (e.g.Dubin 1970). In terms of career structures, the lower value placed upon stability in American organizations is, it is said, reflected in higher rates of job mobility.

A comparison between managers in the British- and American-owned companies located in the advertising, electronics and pharmaceuticals industries appears to lend some support to these observations. Managers in the American-owned companies had generally experienced a greater amount of job mobility during their period of employment with their organizations (Table 4.7). This difference approximates to the 95 per cent level of confidence, and it was also found by Inkson et al. (1970) in their comparison of American and British managers. The level of qualifications held by managers in American-owned firms tended to be higher, though their average ages were not appreciably different.

The data on personal orientations also tend to confirm popular

Table 4.7

Company ownership and managerial characteristics

(Sub-sample of managers in American- and British-owned companies in the advertising, electronics and pharmaceuticals industries)

Variable	Mean scores			
	American ownership $N = 162$	British ownership $N = 230$	Value of t	Level of confidence (P)
Personal background				
1 Age	43·46	44·21	0·96	n.s.
2 Level of qualifications	3·12	2·65	2·07	< 0·05
3 Length of time in organization	11·61	12·63	1·14	n.s.
4 Number of positions held	3·58	3·14	1·95	≐ 0·05
5 Time in present position	3·74	4·37	1·50	n.s.
Personal orientation				
6 Preference for varied work environment	7·62	7·04	2·30	< 0·05
7 Risk-taking	2·12	2·12	0·00	n.s.
8 Expectations on questioning authority	14·68	13·61	1·98	< 0·05
9 Expectations on pressing for change	29·84	28·76	1·06	≐ 0·05

observation. Managers working in the American-owned companies profess a greater preference for a varied working environment and somewhat higher expectations regarding the challenging of authority and pressing for change. However, the differences between the two groups are not large and when the American–British ownership factor is run in a two-way analysis of variance against industry, functional specialism or size of firm, the level of confidence that can be attached to ownership as an independent predictor drops in each case below the 95 per cent level of confidence. In other words, what on the face of things appears to be a corollary of American *versus* British company control turns out to be more a corollary of other differences which happen in our sample to be distributed with some skew towards American ownership. There was, for instance, a relatively large number of American-owned organizations in the advertising sample.

Personal orientations and the role

Managers who express greater preference for variety in the work

Table 4.8

Product–moment correlations between variables of managers' personal background and orientation $N = 787$†

	1	2	3	4	5	6	7	8	9
Personal background									
1 Age	–								
2 Level of qualifications	—22*	–							
3 Length of time in organization	66*	—22*	–						
4 Number of positions held	16*	00	45*	–					
5 Time in present position	49*	—14*	53*	—11	–				
Personal orientation									
6 Preference for varied work environment	—15*	13*	—12*	09	—22*	–			
7 Risk-taking	—09	05	—09	04	—15*	31* (42)			
8 Expectations on questioning authority	—11	11	—07	08	—13*	25* (48)	21* (55)	–	
9 Expectations on pressing for change	—11	05	—06	12*	—17*	18* (46)	15* (45)	34* (54)	–

†Decimal points omitted.   * $P < 0.001$.
Correlations between variables 6–9 inc. shown in parentheses are between the mean scores per organization, where $N = 78$.

environment also tend to see themselves as more willing to take risks, as Table 4.8 shows. Over the sample as a whole the managers who display high personal flexibility along these dimensions are also likely to take the view that they should be prepared to question authority and press for change within their organizations. Their attitudes are therefore relatively consistent in a manner to be expected: those exhibiting a greater personal flexibility tend to be the same people who prefer not to take the *status quo* for granted.

A comparison of the correlations between managers' scores on these variables averaged by organization, shown in parentheses in Table 4.8, confirms that there is a consistent association between our four measures of personal orientation. The fact that the levels of correlation rise is possibly not only an artefact of the aggregation of scores, but also an indication that membership of the same organization imposes a degree of conformity in attitudes among senior personnel. This is likely to be achieved through the processes of managerial selection and development, but may also be encouraged by the nature of managerial roles which in turn reflects the particular organization's task culture. One is reminded here of McMurry's (1958) research among bank employees, where a high degree of consistency was found between their attitudes and the characteristics of banking roles and career structures.

Table 4.9

Product–moment correlations between managers' perceptions of role routine and their personal orientation $N = 787$†

Personal orientation	Perceptions of role routine		
	1 Underlying problems and skills required do not often change	2 Everyday routine	3 Long-term (year-to-year) stability in content of job
1 Preference for varied work environment	—33*	—37*	—18*
2 Risk-taking	—17*	—15*	—16*
3 Expectations on questioning authority	—17*	—12*	—16*
4 Expectations on pressing for change	—16*	—21*	—14*

†Decimal points omitted.   * $P < 0.001$.

One aspect of career history among managers in the present sample was particularly associated with higher scores on all four measures of personal orientation. This is the length of time that managers had spent in their present jobs. Managers who had held their posts for a longer period of time tended to express less preference for variety in work, less propensity towards risk-taking, and they had lower expectations regarding the pursuit of change or the questioning of formal authority. These managers also tended to be older, to have fewer qualifications and to have been longer with their present companies. This set of characteristics described the profile of those managers who seemed to be cautious and conservative and who, perhaps for this reason, had succeeded in achieving a greater degree of accommodation with their organization and with the conditions of their role.

This conclusion is supported by the way in which the managers' perceptions of their roles is associated with their personal orientations (Table 4.9). Three multi-item measures were taken of managers' role perceptions. The first was concerned with the routineness of underlying problems encountered and skills required for their solution in a manager's job. The second was concerned with the degree of everyday routine encountered in his job, in effect the degree of programmed activity. The third measure was of the year-to-year variation in the content of managers' jobs. (These measures are fully described in Child and Ellis, 1973.) The managers who perceived their jobs as being more routine, both in respect of programming and of underlying problems, expressed less desire for variety in their work situation. In addition to this strong relationship, routine in managers' jobs was generally associated with less flexible and more conformist attitudes among the incumbents.

What lies behind these relationships? Although our measures of routine in managerial jobs rely on perceptual data, their predictability from variables such as organization structure, managerial function and career history supports the view that the perceptions are highly consonant with the objective nature of the actual jobs. If this is accepted, then it can be suggested that routine in managers' jobs leads to conservative and conforming attitudes through one or both of two processes. The routine nature of the jobs themselves may over time influence managers to revise their attitudes in a more conservative direction, or managers already possessing such attitudes may over time gravitate towards and remain in relatively routine roles. The alternative hypothesis that managers who have more conservative orientations will regard their roles for this reason as being more routine does not readily appeal to common sense. If anything, one would expect to find the reverse to be true.

Performance and the manager

Comparisons between British and American managers are usually ventured with some reference to the supposedly contrasting levels of performance achieved by their companies. In this way, the personal qualities and philosophies of managers are assumed to contribute in an important manner towards differences in organizational performance.

The performance of the companies in the study was assessed in regard to return and to growth. The three main measures of return employed were percentage income to net assets, percentage income to sales and sales to net assets, annual figures being averaged for the five years up to the date of investigation. Growth was assessed in terms of the percentage growth over the same five years in income, net assets and sales respectively.

Youth among senior management clearly emerged as a correlate of faster organizational growth: the younger the average age of senior managers, the higher the rate of growth, especially in net assets and sales. Correlations with growth data, standardized to eliminate inter-industry differences, were:

Age and income growth   : -0.24, $P < 0.05$ ($N = 72$ companies)
Age and net assets growth: -0.42, $P < 0.001$ ($N = 71$ companies)
Age and sales growth   : -0.42, $P < 0.001$ ($N = 73$ companies).

The relationship between management youth and company growth was evident among companies in each of the six industries studied, although it was relatively weak in chocolate and sweet firms.

While companies with younger managements have on average higher rates of growth, they also exhibit greater variability in growth rates achieved. The higher standard deviations for the group of companies with younger management teams demonstrate this fact in the following data:

	Companies with young managements: average age below sample median of 45·9 years (net assets, $N = 35$ companies) (sales, $N = 37$ companies)	Companies with older managements: average age above sample median of 45·9 years ($N = 36$ companies)
Average standardized score for growth in net assets	53·38	44·93
(standard deviation)	(16·45)	(8·38)
Average standardized score for growth in sales	54·71	44·59
(standard deviation)	(15·53)	(11·69)

Assuming Ns to be equal, and allowing ($N = 1$) degrees of freedom, the level of statistical confidence for the difference in net assets growth means is $P \simeq 0.01$, and for the difference in sales growth means $P < 0.01$.

These results linking younger senior management with higher company growth are very similar in form to those found independently in four British industries by Hart and Mellors (1970). They concluded that 'the growth of companies controlled by senior men is slower, but less volatile'. Some caution is necessary in interpreting these findings since high growth may itself in some degree lead to a younger management rather than the reverse. In conditions of growth more managerial recruits have to be found and these are usually younger men, while the internal promotion of younger men may also be accelerated.

The possibility that high growth, once achieved, leads to a lowering of the average managerial age only received limited support from our data. We found that managers in faster growing companies have had a shorter average length of service in their organization ($r = -0.29$ with sales growth), and they tended to have held a lower number of positions previous to their present posts ($r = -0.23$ with sales growth). A problem with interpreting these results as indicators of accelerated promotion consequent on company growth is that we do not know at what level the managers first entered the organization. The hypothesis that growth leads to managerial youth also suggests that in faster growing companies managers would on average have held their present posts for shorter lengths of time. In fact the correlation between growth (of sales) and average length of present job occupancy is close to zero ($r = -0.06$).

There are, then, some grounds for retaining an open mind on the possibility that younger managers are able to expend more physical and mental effort towards the growth and change of their organizations; in other words that youth promotes growth. Further support for this line of reasoning lies in the finding that younger managements reported a greater tendency at their level to question the formal rules and authority operating in their companies ($r = 0.46$), and a greater pressure for change in general ($r = 0.31$). Younger management teams also believed themselves to be more competent at their jobs ($r = 0.39$).

There was overall no relationship between the average age of managers and the levels of return achieved by a company. The managerial attributes we measured did not appear to be associated with differences in the level of profitability. The only association of any note was the tendency for managements which on average expressed a greater willingness to take risks to be leading companies with higher income to net assets and sales to net assets; but this tendency fell just below the 95 per cent level of statistical confidence. One finding which was expected, in so far as it conforms to the values of a technological society, did not emerge. There was no relationship between the average level of formal qualifications held by management teams and the level of company performance.

The question of causality remains unanswered by these findings. It is worth iterating that managerial characteristics such as relative youth, which are associated with higher levels of company performance, may in part be consequences not causes of that performance. Among the personal orientations of managers which we measured, only their propensity towards risk-taking showed even a modest relationship to performance. It is to be expected that attitudes might in any case be less closely tied to performance than is behaviour, and there are indications from our research that this is indeed so. Also our measures of performance relate to the whole organization, while it has become clear that managerial orientations are to an important degree specific to different functional areas. This is probably a further reason why we have found little connection in our research between the attitudes of managers and the performance of companies.

Conclusion

The results reported in this chapter identify several bases of differentiation in managers' personal backgrounds and in their orientations towards behaviour at work. These findings serve as a point of comparison against which a number of popular managerial stereotypes can be evaluated.

The notion of bureaucratic man cannot, in the light of our data, be fairly attributed to senior managers within the context to which it is generally applied. Indeed, like its close relation 'organization man', the stereotype is too indiscriminate. It is insensitive to the multiple dimensions of organizational roles and their environments which emerge as major referents for predicting variety among managers. More descriptive of our findings are stereotypes of managerial behaviour, careers and orientations which refer to a specific occupational or industrial context. Indeed, the present findings, together with others on the role characteristics of the same sample of managers (cf. Child and Ellis, 1973), lend support to McLennan's (1967) conclusion from a study of American managers that a series of managerial occupations can be said to exist within the broad labour force category of 'manager'

The processes through which managers select, and are selected into, their jobs seem in practice to result in considerable accommodation between the nature of those jobs and the dispositions of the men in them. This much is suggested by the high degree of association which is found between the context of managers' jobs and their expressed personal characteristics. This finding implies that the personal requirements for continued performance in a managerial job are in large part definable only by reference to its context. The advantages which appear to accrue to youth constitute a major exception, but these probably have much more to do with general levels of ability and energy than with particular types of attitude. While youth did correlate with holding more flexible attitudes, this was not a strong relationship, especially when compared with correlations between such attitudes and features of job context. Our broad conclusion is that management selection does, and probably should, rely heavily on the definition of the attitudes and personal background considered appropriate for a particular job in its context, rather than on a generalized stereotype of the 'good manager'. In other words, for the selection of people into managerial positions, organizations should adopt criteria which are 'realistic' to the needs of those positions in their wider organizational context.

This conclusion also has some bearing on the rationale of management education. The main body of management education is located within a framework of standardized courses, the normal unit of entry to which is the individual manager. Managers on such courses are separated from their own operating contexts and placed together with others drawn from a variety of backgrounds. Not only does this procedure rely on the assumption that an organization's performance can be substantially influenced by an individual's achievement and sense of direction, but also that it is appropriate for selected individuals to be educated to match themselves against whatever ideal type is implicit in the main thrust of the course. Our results, and those of similar research, do not seem to lend much support to this philosophy. They suggest, rather, that further investigation of managers' working contexts by management educators is essential in order to test implicit stereotypes more carefully against empirical reality, and to identify those variables within the manager's own environment which contribute to improved performance. This is in effect to support Pym's (1968) view that management development cannot be separated from organizational evaluation as a whole.

PART II
GROUP STUDIES

5 Influence of structure at organizational and group levels*

DIANA C. PHEYSEY, R.L. PAYNE and D.S. PUGH

In his review of the literature on the comparative study of organizations, Udy (1965, p. 706) said that organization theory needed 'attempts on the theoretical plane to develop systematic ways of moving from one level of organizational analysis to another', as, for example, 'from administration to group, to membership effects'. Pugh et al. (1963) also argued that a useful way to analyze organizations was to study them at three levels – the total organization, the small group, and the individual – and to examine the interrelations between them.

Hickson (Chapter 1) in his review of the literature on organization theory found that 'a linear relationship between degree of role prescription and other behaviour variables is almost universally taken for granted', and that several writers supported each of the following relationships: that higher role prescription leads to less confusion, lower anxiety, lower motivation, less innovation, and a decrease in conflict over the exercise of power. The implied value judgement was that low role prescription was better for conditions of change since organizations low on role prescription were more likely to be innovative and to survive and grow. Burns and Stalker (1961), however, pointed out that what they called a mechanistic system of organization, that is, with high role prescription, was likely to be effective in a stable environment. Argyris (1964) too, talked of complex organizational designs, where roles had differing levels of specificity of prescription for differing areas of decision and activity, so that the structure could be varied according to the type of decision faced.

This study asked: (1) Is a difference in the degree of role prescription and in other structural features, notably centralization of authority, accompanied by differences of the kind suggested by Hickson's review article? and (2) How far are conditions at the organizational level

---

* Edited version of a paper originally published in *Administrative Science Quarterly*, vol. 16, 1971, pp. 61–73.

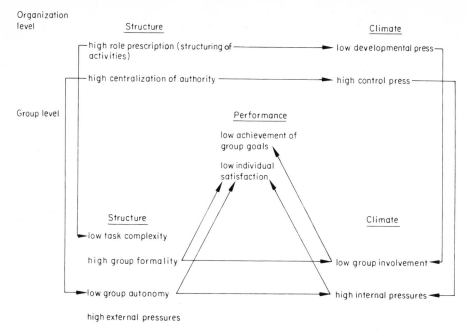

Fig. 5.1 Relationships expected among structure and climate variables in a mechanistic organization

congruent with conditions at the group level? Figure 5.1 details the variables studied and presents the relationships expected to occur in a mechanistic organization with high role prescription.

Theoretical orientation

The rationale for the relationships suggested in Figure 5.1 is as follows:

Organizational structure and organizational climate A mechanistic structuring of activities, through division of labour, standardized procedures and written specification over-prescribes the tasks of managers and is, therefore, not likely to produce a developmental climate where people are stimulated to be innovative. Secondly, the centralization and the high ratio of superordinates characteristic of such organizations are likely to lead to an emphasis on control.

Organizational structure and group structure At the group level, a mechanistic structure is likely to result in low task complexity, especially at lower levels, and in greater formality of relationships, with emphasis on

72

memos, minutes, written instructions and agendas limiting the opportunity for spontaneous, informal communication. Lack of autonomy may accompany the formality, since authority in a mechanistic organization tends to be concentrated at the top of the hierarchy (Burns and Stalker, 1961). These characteristics are not always associated, however, as Pugh et al. (1968) showed. Their measure of structuring of work activities – which included formalization – was independent of centralization of authority.

Organizational climate and group climate Many writers have argued that top executives are likely to have great influence on the climate of the organization, and, once the top policy makers have made decisions, they exert pressure on subordinates to execute them. Members under such pressure and control, who must execute decisions in which they have not participated, are not likely to have a high sense of involvement in the group's activities and goals, and therefore are not likely to take great satisfaction in their work.

Method

Procedures

The procedure for collecting the data in this study was as follows:

1 Information on organizational structure and context was obtained by interviews with senior managers.

2 A sociometric questionnaire was given to line managers and related staff personnel.

3 Interviews were held with members of the selected groups to collect data about their individual jobs, interdependence with other personnel, and individual job satisfaction.

4 Hemphill's (1956) questionnaire on group dimensions was left with members of the groups at the end of these interviews.

5 Further interviews were held with group members about the task structure of group, group atmosphere, perceived pressures on the group, group aims, and so on.

6 The business organizational climate index was left with members of the groups at the end of the interview.

7 Written reports were sent back to all participants.

Measures

The group measures used were as follows, with mean item-analysis values given in parenthesis:

Work group structure
(a) Task complexity: 9 items, related to Shaw's (1963) dimensions each rated for frequency of occurrence on an 8-point scale (0·54).
(b) Formality: Hemphill's (1956) flexibility scale shortened to 8 items and the scoring reversed (0·63).
(c) Autonomy: Hemphill's (1956) autonomy scale shortened to 8 items (0·83).
(d) External pressures: 8-point frequency rating of how often pressure was exerted on the group from five external sources (0·66).

Work group climate
(a) Involvement: Hemphill's (1956) potency scale shortened to 10 items (0·67) and Hemphill's (1956) participation scale shortened to 7 items (0·75).
(b) Internal pressures: 8-point frequency rating in answer to the question 'How often does the group come under pressure from people within the group itself?'

Work group performance
(a) Achievement of subgroup goals: 8-point rating from very successful to very unsuccessful.
(b) Satisfaction with individual members: Cornell job-description index of satisfaction with work, pay, promotion, supervision, and people (Smith et al., 1969).

Sample

Selection of the organizations The research design involved selecting at least two organizations of the same size and the same sort of production process, but otherwise as different as possible. These were given the code names Aston and Brum. Table 5.1 gives details of the differences between them, with reference to the structural variables developed by Pugh et al. (1968, 1969). Scores for the dimensions connected with structuring of activities and concentration of authority were standardized on a sample of 52 Birmingham, England, organizations employing 240–25,000 employees (Pugh et al., 1968). The standard score mean = 50 and standard deviation = 15; the configuration scores are raw scores. Aston employed 350 people compared to Brum's 412 and was part of a

Table 5.1

Scores on dimensions of organization structure

Structure	Aston	Brum
Structuring of activities	59	40
Standardization of procedures	66	39
Formalization of role performance records	56	45
Formalization	68	39
Role specialization (nonproduction jobs)	46	44
Concentration of authority	48	28
Lack of autonomy (to make decisions)	53	33
Centralization	43	21
Configuration		
Vertical span (height of hierarchy)	5	8
Percentage of line superordinates to total personnel	5·4%	3·6%
Percentage of nonproduction personnel to total personnel	52·0%	26·0%
Percentage of clerks to total personnel	14·0%	7·6%
Number of subordinates (first-line supervisors)	12	38
Size of organization	350	412

large international corporation. It had acquired many standard procedures from the parent company, and its score was well above Brum's on structuring of activities. For example, it had daily stock control, an induction programme for new employees, and programmed machine maintenance, all lacking in Brum. Hence the different scores of the two companies on standardization of procedures. Aston was also very formalized in comparison with the mean for the sample population on which scores were standardized (Pugh et al., 1968), even though most of these organizations had many more employees than Aston. It had, for example, written terms of reference for all levels and duplicated agendas for meetings, whereas Brum did not.

The scores on role specialization of nonproduction jobs were similar. Both organizations scored below the mean for the original sample population, but for different reasons. For an activity to be scored as specialized there had to be at least one person employed in it full time by the organization. In Aston's case, personnel from headquarters provided certain specialized services but these did not contribute to the specialization

75

score because these specialists were not employed at the Aston site. Aston did, however, have research and development, data processing and auditing as internal specialisms, but it had no local sales force. Brum, on the other hand, had sales personnel, but no research and development, data processing, or auditing specialisms. Brum employed mainly generalists, and scored low for this reason.

Aston scored 68 and Brum 39 on a measure of dependence on other organizations and institutions. As might be expected from the strong correlation between dependence and centralization (Pugh et al., 1969), Aston had much less autonomy than Brum and was relatively more centralized internally, although slightly less centralized than the mean for the organizations in the orginal sample. Brum, however, had a score two standard deviations below the mean on centralization. Its supervisors, for example, had full authority for hiring and firing, and its managers had authority for policy decisions on marketing, whereas Aston supervisors and managers did not have comparable authority.

Selection of the groups Line management and supervisory groups were chosen because it was felt that they would be most likely to show the effects of structure. Members of the groups, listed in Table 5.2 were chosen on the basis of an analysis of a sociometric questionnaire (see Chapter 6). The groups in Aston corresponded exactly to the formal organization chart. In Brum, however, according to the organization chart, the top management consisted of the chief executive, the company secretary, the commercial manager and the works manager; middle management included the assistant works manager, the works engineer and one departmental manager. On the basis of the questionnaire, however, the works engineer was not seen as a member of the middle-management group, and the works manager, the assistant works manager and the departmental manager were seen as being in both the top and middle management. These deviations seem to reflect the lack of attention paid to formal charts, and were presumably the result of a general lack of concern with rules and procedures in a nonbureaucratic organization. These results are reported in full in Chapter 6.

Results

Organizational structure and organizational climate

The results of this aspect of the study are reported in Chapter 7.

Table 5.2
Composition of production group

Aston	Brum
Top-management groups	
1 plant manager	1 managing director
1 personnel manager	1 works manager
1 planning superintendent	1 assistant works manager
1 industrial engineer	1 company secretary
3 technical managers	1 commercial manager
1 general production superintendent	1 departmental production manager
	1 works engineer
Middle-management groups	
1 general production superintendent	1 works manager
4 departmental production superintendents	1 assistant works manager
	2 departmental managers
	1 metallurgist
	4 production section managers
	1 transport manager
First-line supervisory groups	
1 departmental production superintendent	1 departmental manager
2 production foremen (1 on each shift)	1 assistant manager
	1 foreman
or	
8 production foremen (4 on each shift)	1 assistant foreman

Organizational structure and group structure

Mechanistic structure and task complexity of lower participants It was hypothesized, following Melman (1958), that structuring of activities and centralization of authority would simplify tasks, especially those of participants lower in the organizational hierarchy. Table 5.3 shows the scores on group structure variables. In Aston, managerial groups saw themselves as having slightly more complex tasks than the supervisory

Table 5.3

Structural variables and perceptions of organizational and group climate

| | Aston | | | | | | Brum | | | | | |
| | Median scores of groups | | | | Statistics computed from individual scores | | Median scores of groups | | | Statistics computed from individual scores | | Significant intercompany differences |
Variables	Top management	Middle management	Supervisory N = 3	Supervisory N = 9	Mean	SD	Top management	Middle management	Supervisory	Mean	SD	p
Task complexity	39	39	36	29	36·7	8·7	28	32	37	34·0	9·9	—
Informality versus formality	20	21	19	22	20·5	4·6	31	29	30	29·5	3·9	<·05
Autonomy	31	30	22	25	26·4	5·6	45	44	33	40·6	7·5	<·05
External pressures	16	23	22	15	19·8	4·8	7	9	24	11·7	4·6	<·05
Developmental press	110	109	110	114	109·2	7·4	108	108	104	102·7	9·6	<·05
Involvement	86	69	81	73	78·6	12·0	65	60	71	66·3	15·1	<·05
Normative control	101	107	101	96	102·9	7·3	96	96	105	99·5	8·3	—
Internal pressures	6	6	3	4	4·8	1·8	3	6	6	5·2	2·3	—

groups, the difference being significant at the 6 per cent level of confidence using a one-tailed Mann-Whitney U-test, whereas in Brum the medians indicated that the group lowest in the hierarchy saw itself as having the most complex task. In fact, the medians are slightly misleading because statistically there were no differences among the three Brum groups. Apparently the lack of standard procedures and formalized routines in Brum did lead to complex tasks for groups at all levels. There was only a very small absolute difference in the mean degree of perceived task complexity between the two companies, as Table 5.3 shows, but Aston employees saw their tasks as being slightly more complex. From the authors' knowledge of the company, the high score on task complexity for the supervisory group in Brum was not surprising, since the group was one of two major production units of the company and at the time of study had the major responsibility for producing a profit. Thus, the combination of procedures and centralized decision making in Aston reduced the complexity of jobs lower in the organization, but made jobs at the top of the organization more complex. Indeed, the complexity of the administrative system itself may have contributed to this. The lack of standardization at Brum and the considerable amount of responsibility delegated even to the lowest level meant that the lowest group's task was complex.

Mechanistic structure and group formality It was hypothesized that there would be less informality at the group level in Aston, which had higher structuring of activities, and the hypothesis was supported. The scores for informality and formality shown in Table 5.3 indicate that, although there was little difference in scores within each company, Aston groups were much less informal than Brum groups, with Aston mean score almost 30 per cent lower than that of Brum.

Mechanistic structure and group autonomy It was hypothesized that Aston groups would have less perceived group autonomy than would Brum groups because of Aston's higher score on centralization of authority, and the hypothesis was supported. Table 5.3 shows that the score on perceived group autonomy for top management in Aston was even lower than that of the bottom group in Brum. In Aston top management had to refer certain decisions to the parent company, whereas in Brum the board of directors allowed considerable freedom in decision making to the executive directors, who were members of Brum's top-management group.

Mechanistic structure and external pressures It was hypothesized that centralization of authority would lead to external pressures on the group. The external pressures score for Aston (19·8) was much higher than for

Brum (11·7), as Table 5.3 shows. Furthermore, Aston groups seemed to feel a similar degree of external pressure, whereas in Brum felt pressure was greater at the bottom of the hierarchy. This accords with the findings on the complexity of the task in the supervisory group in Brum. The low score on external pressure of the middle group in Brum may have resulted partly from the fact that the leader of the group, the works manager, was a director of the firm and also a member of the top-management group. Centralized structures and being low in the organizational hierarchy seem to lead to a perceived lack of autonomy and a feeling of being under pressure from outside the immediate work group.

Organizational climate and group climate

The measure of organizational climate used in this study is described in Chapter 7. It consisted of twenty-four scales adding up to a total of 254 items, each of which had to be described as true or false. A principal components analysis of the twenty-four scales reduced them to two main components and these were used to compare Aston and Brum in the present paper. The two factors were:

Developmental press which describes the degree to which the organization is concerned with the development of scientific, technical and administrative procedures as well as with the development of its employees.

Normative control which measures the degree to which the climate of the organization emphasizes following rules and procedures, keeping to conventions and maintaining control of one's emotions. Senior management particularly keep themselves at a distance from other employees in organizations which have a climate strong on this factor. Chapter 7 describes how these two climate factors relate to the climate in the managerial groups in the two organizations.

Developmental press and group involvement It was hypothesized that involved groups would be more likely to be found where there was developmental press, because management concern for employee involvement was one of the scales with a high loading on the developmental and progressive factor in the business organizational climate index. There was a relationship between perceptions of developmental press in the organization and perceptions of the degree of involvement among group members, as Table 5.3 shows, the rank-order correlation being 0·76 ($p < 0.05$); however, when a second-order partial product–moment correlation was calculated, partialling out for individual perceptions of climate and group involvement, the correlation between

80

the group scores dropped to 0·25 (NS). Thus, members who saw the organizational climate as being developmental also tended to see their group as being involved, but when groups were taken as the unit of analysis, the common variance between the two measures was considerably reduced. Nevertheless, as the means for the two companies on group involvement show that Aston had a higher level of perceived group involvement, the bureaucratic formulation shown in Figure 5.1, which would give Aston low developmental press and low group involvement, was not supported at the group level, any more than it was at the organizational level.

Normative control pressure and internal group pressures It was hypothesized that in a climate that emphasized rules and regulations there would be pressure exerted in the group to comply with standards and achieve targets and therefore higher perceived internal group pressures. There was very weak support for this hypothesis; with individual perceptions held constant, the second-order partial correlation between the group scores was only 0·31(NS).

Group structure and group climate

Mechanistic structure and group involvement It was hypothesized that Aston's more mechanistic structure, associated with greater formality at the group level, would be associated with lower group involvement, but the hypothesis was not supported. All Aston groups were more formal and had members who felt a higher degree of involvement in the groups' activities, the zero-order correlation between formality and involvement being 0·82 ($p < 0.05$), though this dropped to 0·60 (NS) when individual scores were held constant. This positive association between group formality and group involvement at subunit level parallels that found between structuring of activities and developmental press at the organizational level.

Mechanistic structure and internal group pressures It was hypothesized that the combination of formal interpersonal relations, low group autonomy and high external pressures would lead to greater felt internal pressures, but these structural factors seemed to have no relationship with intragroup processes in this study. Presumably, factors such as interpersonal compatibility were more influential in determining felt pressures within the group. The supervisory groups in Aston suffered most severely from structural constraints, as Table 5.3 shows, but they had the lowest scores on felt internal pressures.

It was hypothesized, as Figure 5.1 suggests, that in mechanistic organizations low task complexity, high formality, low autonomy and high external pressures would lead to low satisfaction, and consequently poor performance, but the hypothesis was not supported. Although an attempt was made to obtain ratings of group performance in terms of goal attainment, membership replaceability and ability to work together, there was very little variance on these measures. Individual satisfaction was conceived as a group output in the sense that the immediate work group ought to be a major determinant of members' satisfactions. Table 5.4 presents the correlations for group structure and climate variables with each of the five aspects of job satisfaction measured by the Cornell job description index for 7 groups, with total individual responses involved varying from 37 to 42. The second-order partial correlations – controlling for individual perceptions of structure, climate and satisfaction variables – hold the individual scores constant and measure the remaining degree of relationship between the median group scores. It was expected that satisfaction with work and with supervision would be affected and possibly with co-workers too but not with pay and promotion.

None of the second-order partial correlations was significant at the 5 per cent level of confidence; and, where they were of any size, they fail to bear out the prediction. None of the structural variables had any relationship at all with satisfaction with work itself. Members were, unexpectedly, more dissatisfied with supervision (—0·52) when the task was complex; perhaps the supervisor became a scapegoat for personal problems and difficulties.

Satisfaction with co-workers was higher, not lower, in the more formal Aston groups. Perhaps the measure of satisfaction with co-workers might

Table 5.4

Correlations of group structure and climate with group satisfaction

Variables	Work		Pay		Promotion		Supervision		Co-workers	
	Zero order	Second order	Zero order	Second order	Zero order	Second order	Zero order	Second order	Zero order	Second order
Task complexity	·22	—·07	—·18	—·13	·18	—·03	—·55	—·52	—·12	—·29
Automony	—·01	—·13	·33	·49	—·39	—·28	—·22	—·01	—·23	—·02
Formality	·38	·16	—·02	—·04	·73*	·48	·01	·05	·71*	·62
Involvement	·24	·18	·12	—·11	·70	·59	·16	·29	·64	·45
Internal pressures	·78*	·72	·35	·03	·32	·22	—·40	—·25	·23	·10

* p < ·05

be better named esteem, because the question asked whether those with whom the respondent worked were active, ambitious, boring, intelligent, responsible, slow, smart, stimulating, stupid, and so on. This correlation might have arisen because members in Aston (1) were more educated, most of the top-management group in Aston being graduates, whereas none of Brum's top-management group was; (2) had job experience in other organizations, whereas most Brum managers had not; and (3) were younger than Brum managers by about 10 years. Thus, the type of esteem implied by the items in this scale might appropriately be applied to Aston managers. The Aston groups were also more satisfied with their promotion prospects, which were much better, since Aston was part of a large international corporation. In fact, during the study's three months in the factory, three of the sample were promoted.

Group climate and group performance

It was hypothesized that involvement would be positively correlated with satisfaction with work, supervision and co-workers, but only the last of these relationships was supported. The high correlation between involvement and satisfaction with promotion opportunities was again related to the Aston groups being the most involved and having the best promotion prospects.

It was hypothesized that groups with high internal pressures would have lower satisfaction with work, supervision, and co-workers. There was slight support for lower satisfaction with supervision. The relationship with satisfaction with work was quite strong, but in the opposite direction to that predicted. This was very much a group relationship, for the correlation between internal pressures and satisfaction with work for the 42 individuals was only 0·17. Perhaps the pressures were not those of conflict, but those for achievement, and where a group is able to establish these it leads to satisfaction with work through a sense of challenge.

The two or three hours of interviews with each manager and supervisor reinforced the findings from the questionnaires. The differences in the organizational structuring of activities were strongly reflected in the way people responded to the instruction 'please describe your job and what it entails'. Only 73 per cent ($N = 15$) of the Aston personnel mentioned production planning and scheduling, compared to 92 per cent ($N = 12$) in Brum. Similarly, dealing with materials, stocks and supplies was mentioned by 75 per cent of Brum managers and supervisors, and only 50 per cent in Aston. On the other hand, 87 per cent of Aston personnel reported spending time on record keeping and administration, in contrast to the 50 per cent at Brum. Perhaps more surprisingly, however, nobody in Brum mentioned dealing with personal problems of employees, while 33 per cent mentioned it at Aston, which seems to reflect Aston's very conscious concern with their employees' welfare and involvement in the company.

This is also reflected in the differences in response to the question: 'Can you say whether you all, as a group, have common aims which are specifically related to your work?' In Aston, more members reported things like developing people, communicating with people, safety and human relations, as well as increasing efficiency, improving quality, and ensuring a smooth flow of work. In Brum members tended to refer to a more general goal of working for the growth and benefit of the company. There were no differences in the frequency with which reducing costs, making a profit, and improving production were mentioned. Altogether, these kinds of comments seem to support the questionnaire data, in that Aston members seemed much more conscious of actively managing the material aspects of the workflow, the administrative aspects, and indeed the personnel aspects. The fact that one can set up administrative systems for facilitating the resolution of human as well as material problems seems to have been neglected in the consideration of the effects of the mechanistic system of organization.

Conclusions

This study explored the relationships between organizational structure and organizational climate across two levels – the whole organization and line subgroups within it.

Organization structure in the two organizations was consistently related to group structure. High role prescription, or structuring of activities, was associated with high group formality at all levels, and with lower task complexity for lower-level groups. High centralization of authority was associated with low group autonomy and high external pressures. Similarly, organizational climate was consistently related to group climate. Low developmental press was associated with low group involvement, and high control press with high internal pressures.

The relationships found between organizational structure and organizational and group climates were more complex. Although the hypothesized relation between high concentration of authority and high control press was supported for rules orientation and conventionality, high structuring of activities was not associated with low developmental press at the organizational level, nor with low group involvement at the group level.

It is not possible from an exploratory study of this kind to say whether the different climates found at organizational and group level in the two organizations were in any sense caused by the marked differences between the two structures. It can only be said that the dysfunctions attributed to bureaucracy (March and Simon, 1958) were not found in Aston. Aston was not a perfect example of Weber's ideal-type bureaucracy – nor were Selznick's (1957) TVA, Gouldner's (1955) gypsum mine, or Burns and Stalker's (1961) mechanistic factories, where the dysfunctions of bureaucracy were originally noted.

Organizational structure is multidimensional, as the four conceptually orthogonal factors found by Pugh et al. (1968) indicate, and the behavioural consequences of one aspect of organizational structure can be negated by the effect of another. Thus an organization with a tall, vertical, hierarchy in which lower levels have authority to make decisions may have low participation in practice because of regard to status differentials. The advantages of decentralization are nullified, as for example in Brum. Similarly, an organization with quite extreme scores on some aspects of bureaucracy could produce a stimulating and progressive climate, given the support from other aspects of its structure. For example, Aston had management appraisal and promotion procedures expressly oriented toward the development of its members.

Organizational climate is also multidimensional. As Payne and Pheysey show in Chapter 7, 24 possible characteristics did not discriminate uniformly between the two organizations with their differing structures. Both Aston and Brum were high on sociability and low on interpersonal aggression in spite of their large differences on other aspects of climate. Furthermore, the relationships between organizational structure and behavioural and attitudinal variables such as organizational climate are complicated by differential effects at varying job levels. In this study, perceived group autonomy decreased down the organizational hierarchy in Aston, but was similar at all levels in Brum. In a study of over 280 senior managers in 40 organizations, Inkson et al. (1968) found that executives at the top of structured, that is, bureaucratic, organizations saw their jobs as being less clearly defined and less routine than those of senior executives in unstructured organizations, and expected colleagues to be more innovative and less conforming. Child's paper (Chapter 3) elaborates these results. However, it could be that the bureaucratization of jobs lower in the hierarchy leaves senior management free to attempt more complex and innovative tasks, and that the classic dysfunctions of bureaucracy exist largely at lower levels. The data on Aston show that dysfunctions do not necessarily exist even at lower levels, though, as has already been suggested, this is probably due to the moderating effect of structural variables such as having fewer hierarchical levels and being relatively small, and to nonstructural variables such as having a young, well-educated management.

Theorists have neglected the relevance of such an obvious factor as level in the job hierarchy. The fact that organismic structures seem to lead to more flexible and innovative behaviour amongst middle and senior managers is extrapolated to describe the behaviour of all members of the organization. Similarly, management writers such as Taylor (1947) and Fayol (1949) developed their ideas in trying to solve the problem of how to control and standardize the behaviour of members who are essentially low or intermediate in the organizational hierarchy, but their reasoning has been extended to an analysis of senior management.

Friedlander (1970, p.137) noted the same problem: 'The vast majority of literature relating organizational structure to task accomplishment fails to describe the human, task, or environmental conditions under which a specific structure maximizes task accomplishment. The result of this failure is that two sets of theories and practices have emerged (mechanistic and organismic) each of which occurs in and depends upon – but does not specify – the very different sets of conditions under which that theory and practice are valid.' Friedlander (1970) also pointed out that Burns and Stalker (1961) did refer to environmental conditions in terms of stability and change, but there are obviously many other conditioning factors. Job level is clearly one of those important qualifying conditions; job function – that is, line or staff – and type of personnel – that is, professional or nonprofessional – are others.

The degree of such variables as structuring of activities and concentration of authority is all-important. Hickson (Chapter 1) found it disconcerting that so much thinking had been patterned by a one-dimensional view of bureaucratic structure and its associated dysfunctions of climate. The determination of the degree of a structural characteristic appropriate to an organization's tasks, size, technology and personnel would appear to be more fruitful than the general acceptance of a linear relationship between degree of role prescription and inhibitive behavioural characteristics. This paper suggests further examination of the interrelationship of structure and climate, both viewed multi-dimensionally, in promoting organizational viability.

6 Organization structure and sociometric nominations amongst line managers in three contrasted organizations*

ROY L. PAYNE and DIANA C. PHEYSEY

Given that one accepts the notion of 'organization design', it seems logical to assume that different designs (structures) are accompanied by differences in behaviour and attitudes. Much theory – perhaps more accurately 'armchair speculation' – exists, but there is a shortage of empirical data to support or contradict the theories. Reference to a literature review by Porter and Lawler (1965) indicates that, even where there are comparative studies, there is generally insufficient detail in the descriptions of the organizations being compared, so that one wonders just what the differences are, and how great they are.

The development of measures of organization structure (and its context) by Pugh et al. (1968 and 1969), however, provides a means for selecting organizations with structures of particular types. It is then possible to look for the behavioural concomitants of those structures. The research reported here uses these measures (seven of which are shown in the appendix) to contrast three organizations: one small and somewhat mechanistic[1] in structure; one large and mechanistic; and one small with scarcely any mechanistic features.

As this is one of the few comparative sociometric studies known to us, and the only one involving three carefully contrasted organizations, it must be regarded as exploratory. As Udy (1965) noted, at the present stage of development of organization theory, almost all research is by definition exploratory, and it is inevitable that this should be so. We shall not, therefore, attempt to review existing theory, but shall refer to it where appropriate.

---

* originally published in the *European Journal of Social Psychology,* vol. 1, 1971, pp. 261–84.

The sections of the chapter will be ordered as follows:

1 The three organizations
2 The research procedure
3 Organizationally defined groups and sociometrically defined groups
4 Group size and intra-group choices
5 Hierarchical level of group and nominations upwards, downwards, and to peers
6 The total line management hierarchy, and nominations upwards and downwards
7 External departments and lateral choices
8 Mechanistic structure, line management hierarchy, and sociometric indices
9 Summary and conclusions

1 The three organizations

On the basis of the measures of organization structure already referred to, we selected three manufacturing companies, code-named Carrs, Aston, and Brum.[2] Carrs is the large manufacturing division (2,912 employees) of a structurally mechanistic organization. It has an eight-level hierarchy. Aston, like Carrs, has many mechanistic features, but it is much smaller (350 employees) and flatter (five levels). It manufactures one complete product range for the large international group of which it is a part. Both Carrs and Aston employ a high proportion of supportive (nonproduction) personnel. Brum (412 employees) shares Aston's small size, but it has an eight-level hierarchy, like Carrs. It does not, however, employ many support personnel, nor does it possess any other mechanistic features. It is an independent company, not part of some larger concern. Detailed scores are given in the Appendix.

2 The research procedure

Within each company questionnaires were distributed which asked about interactions, influence, and grouping.[3]

The instructions for the three parts of the questionnaire were as follows:

(A) *Interaction* 'Think back over the past month, consider all the people in your department, i.e., your supervisors, your subordinates, and people at the same level as yourself. Please write down the names of those with whom you have spent most time on most work matters. List the names in order, so that the first person is the one with whom you have spent most time.' There were columns for name, job title, level of job of nominee compared with respondent's job level (that is, higher, same, or lower), nominee's normal place of work, and the frequency of the contact. Respondents were then asked to carry out the same procedure for all people outside their department, and then there was provision for these two lists to be amalgamated so that all nominees were rank-ordered according to amount of time spent with the respondent.[4]

(B) *Influence and advice* 'Would you now think about the people who would be most likely to influence you in work matters, i.e., people whose opinions and advice you would both seek and respect. List them in order, starting with the name of the person whose opinions and advice would in general be of most value to you.'

(C) *Perception of group membership* 'When people work together they quite often form, or are formed, into teams or groups, either because the work to be done requires more than one person to do it, or because people like each other and just enjoy working together, or both. Do you see yourself as a member of any teams or groups of this kind? If you do, please write down the name of all other members of such teams or groups. If you can give the team or group a name, please do so.' Enough space for the description of four groups was available to the respondents.[5]

3 Organizationally defined groups and sociometrically defined groups

One way of defining group boundaries in organizations is to obtain an organization chart, and define the groups as consisting of the occupant of any node on the chart, plus all the people who report to that node. The occupants of nodal positions are, of course, leaders in their own group, and members of some superordinate group, or 'linking-pins', as in Likert's (1961) terms. The question is whether these organizationally defined groups are sociometrically perceived as groups.[6]

Three types of data will be presented here to establish the groupings: (a) perceptions of common membership; (b) interactions and influence; and (c) functional relationships.

(a) *Perceptions of common membership*

Figures 6.1, 6.2 and 6.3 show the organizational charts for Carrs, Aston and Brum respectively, and the groups which would exist (according to

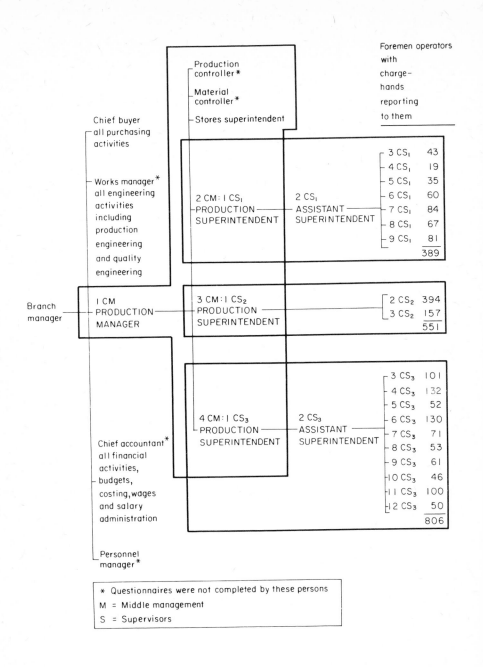

Foremen operators with charge-hands reporting to them

Production controller*
Material controller*
Stores superintendent

Chief buyer
all purchasing activities

Works manager*
all engineering activities including production engineering and quality engineering

2 CM : 1 CS₁ PRODUCTION SUPERINTENDENT	2 CS₁ ASSISTANT SUPERINTENDENT	3 CS₁	43
		4 CS₁	19
		5 CS₁	35
		6 CS₁	60
		7 CS₁	84
		8 CS₁	67
		9 CS₁	81
			389

Branch manager

1 CM PRODUCTION MANAGER

3 CM : 1 CS₂ PRODUCTION SUPERINTENDENT	2 CS₂	394
	3 CS₂	157
		551

Chief accountant*
all financial activities, budgets, costing, wages and salary administration

4 CM : 1 CS₃ PRODUCTION SUPERINTENDENT	2 CS₃ ASSISTANT SUPERINTENDENT	3 CS₃	101
		4 CS₃	132
		5 CS₃	52
		6 CS₃	130
		7 CS₃	71
		8 CS₃	53
		9 CS₃	61
		10 CS₃	46
		11 CS₃	100
		12 CS₃	50
			806

Personnel manager*

* Questionnaires were not completed by these persons
M = Middle management
S = Supervisors

Fig. 6.1 Formally designated 'groups' superimposed on Carrs organization chart

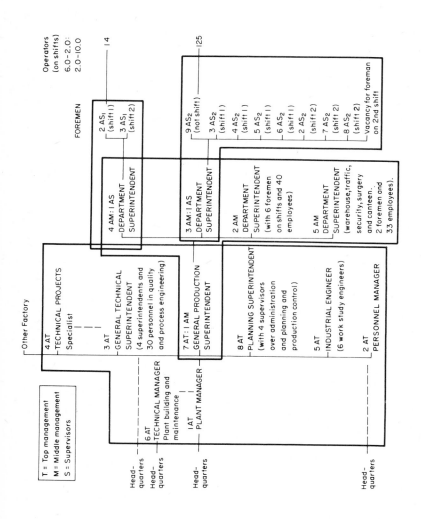

Fig. 6.2 Formally designated 'groups' superimposed on Aston organization chart

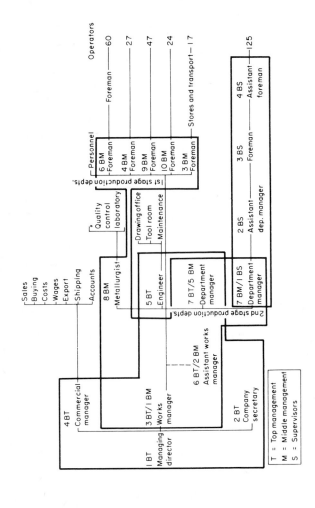

Fig. 6.3 Sociometrically designated 'groups' superimposed on Brum organization chart

the above definition of a group) are outlined. Each member is given a coding according to the group to which he is said to belong.

Figure 6.1 shows, for Carrs, four groups; a middle management group (CM), and three supervisory groups (CS1, CS2, and CS3). Figure 6.2 shows, for Aston, four groups; a top management group (AT), a middle management group (AM), and two supervisory groups (AS1 and AS2). Figure 6.3 shows, for Brum, a top management group (BT), a middle

Table 6.1
Formally defined and perceived group memberships in three manufacturing organizations

	CARRS	ASTON	BRUM
Number of line management studied [a]	22	20	13

	No. of members in formally defined group and perceived group [b]	No. naming formally defined group and perceived group total no. completed questionnaires	%
CM	7	3/4	75
CS1	9	4/6	66
CS2	3	1/3	33
CS3	12	2/12	16
AT	7	6/7	85
AM	5	4/5	80
AS1	3	1/3	33
AS2	8	5/8	62

	No. of members in formally defined group	No. of members in perceived group	No. naming formally defined group/total no. of completed questionnaires	%	No. naming perceived group/total no. completed questionnaires	%
BT	4	7	0/4	0	5/6	83
BM	12	10	0/9	0	4/7	57
BS	4	4	2/4	50	2/4	50

(a) Total respondents are fewer than the completed questionnaires by group, because of some dual memberships.
(b) Job titles and positions are shown in Figures 6.1, 6.2 and 6.3.

C = Carrs
A = Aston
B = Brum
T = Top management
M = Middle management
S = Supervisors

management group (BM), and a supervisory group (BS).

Close inspection of Figures 6.1 and 6.2 shows that the codings coincide with the boundaries drawn. The two bureaucracies have formalized their membership so that those who name the group are agreed upon where the boundaries lie.

Figure 6.3 shows the 'sociometrically' designated groups in Brum, and they are clearly different from the groups represented in the organization chart, assuming the definition that a group comprises the occupant of a nodal position plus the occupant of all positions reporting to that node.

The engineer, whom one would expect to be in the middle group, is said to be in the top group only. The assistant works manager and a department manager have membership in the top group as well as in the middle group. The personnel manager does not have membership in either group. Thus, the perceived membership of the Brum top group is larger than that expected from the chart, and the perceived membership of the middle group is smaller. Table 6.1 gives further details. The table indicates that there is much greater consensus in the top groups, AT and BT, about who is in the groups. For CM and AM, 75 per cent or more of

Table 6.2
Intra-group interactions of formally designated work teams

Group	N	Possible number of mutual interactions	Actual number of nominations	%
CARRS				
CM	4	12	9	75
CS1	9($-$3)[a]	30	17	57
CS2	3	6	5	83
CS3	12	132	42	32
ASTON				
AT	8($-$1)	42	24	57
AM	5	20	14	70
AS1	3	6	5	83
AS2	9($-$1)	56	30	53

BRUM	Formal group	Perceived group	Formal group	Perceived group	Formal group	Perceived group	Formal group	Perceived group
BT	4	6	12	30	17	19	58	63
BM	11($-$4)	7	42	42	16	16	38	38
BS	4	4	12	12	12	12	100	100

[a] Figures in brackets represent the number who did not complete a questionnaire. Calculation is based on remaining members as if they were the only members of the group. Thus if A had not completed a questionnaire, but B mentioned A, that mention was not included.

94

the members name the group and all its members, though in BM, which includes people of four hierarchical levels (and, therefore, some relatively low in the hierarchy), the percentage agreement is lower. For supervisory groups, the maximum percentage is 66 per cent, and in one case it falls below 33 per cent. In view of the fact that spontaneous mention of the group and all its members is less than 100 per cent[7], are there other data to support the groupings as coded?

(b) *Interactions and influence*

When we take into account any mention of a contact[8] it is possible to compare the maximum possible intra-group mentions (using the suggested boundaries) with the actual number of intra-group mentions. This gives a good indication of the degree to which group members see each other. Table 6.2 shows that a good deal of intra-group interaction takes place in groups at all levels, but especially in the smaller groups (CM, CS2, AS1 and BS).

As one might expect, people contacted more other people in the course

Table 6.3
Intra-group influence nominations of formally designated work teams

Group	Possible number of mutual nominations[a]		Actual number of nominations		%		% nominations with leaders' mentions (given and received) excluded	
CM	12		7		58		50	
CS1	30		6		20		15	
CS2	6		4		67		0	
CS3	132		17		13		7	
AT	42		18		43		47	
AM	20		9		45		25	
AS1	6		1		17		0	
AS2	56		9		16		7	
	Formal group	Perceived group	Formal group	Perceived group	Formal group	Perceived group	Formal group	Perceived group
BT	12	30	7	17	58	57	33	50
BM	42	42	7	7	17	17	13	13
BS	12	12	6	6	50	50	17	17

[a] Calculation is based on members who completed questionnaires as if they were the only members of the group. Thus, if A had not completed a questionnaire, but B mentioned A, that mention was not included.

Table 6.4
Results of the task analysis

ASTON

Respondent's code number	AT							AM			AS₁			AS₂								
	1	2	3	4	5	6	8*	1*	2	5	1	2	3	1*	2	3	4	5	6	7	8	9
AT1	–	M	V		M	L	V	V														
AT2		–	L		M		L															
AT3			–	V	L	L	M	M														
AT4				–				M														
AT5					–		M	M														
AT6						–	L	L														
AT8							–	V	M	V	M											
AT7 / AM1								–	V	V	V			V								
AM2									–	M	M			M								
AM5										–												
AM4; / $AS1_1$											–	V	V									
$AS1_2$												–	V									
$AS1_3$													–									
AM3 / $AS2_1$														–	V	V	V	V	V	V	V	V
$AS2_2$															–							
$AS2_3$																–	V	L		V		
$AS2_4$																	–	M	M			L
$AS2_5$																		–	M	M	M	M
$AS2_6$																			–			L
$AS2_7$																				–		
$AS2_8$																					–	
$AS2_9$																						–

BRUM

Respondent's code number	BT				BM'		BM				BS			
	1	2	4	3*	2*	5	3	6	9	10	1*	2	3	4
BT1	–	V	V	V	M									
BT2		–	V											
BT4			–	V							M			
BM1 / BT3				–	V	V					M			
BM2 / BT6					–	V	L	V	V					
BM5 / BT7						–	L		L					
BM3							–	L	M	M				
BM6								–	V					
BM9									–	L				
BM10										–				
BS1											–	V	V	V
BS2												–	V	V
BS3													–	V
BS4														–

V = very important
M = moderately important
L = least important
blank = no interaction mentioned

* = liaison person
——— = segment division as described by Weiss (1956)
- - - = alternative segment division

of their work than they would turn to for help and advice. It is not surprising, therefore, that, for influence, the percentage of actual intra-group nominations to possible intra-group nominations is lower than it is for interaction. Table 6.3 gives details for the groups when the leader is included (the N for each group is the same as shown in Table 6.2), and when the leader is excluded (the N is then reduced by 1). It can be seen that, in the lower groups particularly, most of the nominations to persons inside the groups are directed to the leader. Sometimes supervisors in the two bureaucracies, Carrs and Aston, nominated a person outside their group, often a staff specialist, as the person whose opinions they would seek out and respect.

The higher intra-group influence within CM, AT, and BT is partly determined by the fact that there are fewer external people of equivalent or higher status by whom they are likely to be influenced.

(c) *Functional relationships*

A further perspective on the groupings for Aston and Brum was obtained from interviews in each of these two companies. Each member of the seven groups was asked to give a description of the work he did. The manager and the interviewer then together compiled a list of activities from the descriptions provided. The group member was then asked to rate the degree of importance he attached to each activity from least, through moderately, to most important. Next, he was asked which other persons, if any, were involved with him in each activity. Table 6.4 presents the results of the task analysis, using reciprocated mentions only as recommended by Weiss and Jacobson (1955).

As Table 6.4 shows, people in all groups in both organizations report having tasks which cluster around other members of the groups as we have already defined them (note how a fairly solid matrix of choices occurs for each group), and that these tasks are regarded as being 'very important' or 'moderately important' parts of their own total job responsibilities. The interactions all have functional relevance.

In addition to the information about people's jobs, we wanted to collect other data about the seven groups. Before we asked for any of these data, each person was given a card on which his name appeared, together with the names of all the other members of the group. He was asked to say whether these people constituted a work team, and if he felt able to answer questions about that group of people as a group. None of the people interviewed disagreed with the groups defined by us.

The information presented in Tables 6.1 to 6.4 suggests that at Carrs and

Aston we may take the groups defined by the organization charts as a basis for analysis. At Brum, the groups perceived by respondents seem to provide a slightly better basis, and will be used in further analysis. The more systematic organization in the two bureaucracies seems to work, in that perceived groups are congruent with the formal organization chart, suggesting organization structure affects behaviour in this limited way at least.

4 Group size and intra-group choices

Attention has already been drawn to the fact that the smaller groups tend to have somewhat more intra-group interaction and influence choices. Thomas (1959) showed that such a relationship is to be expected. In our study, the rank order correlations for the eleven groups were: (a) for size of group and interaction nominations = —0·87, and (b) for size of group and intra-group influence nominations = —0·65.

The *frequency* with which people contacted other members of their own groups was *not,* however, affected by whether the group was large or small. (The correlation between size of group and frequency of intra-group interactions per week = 0·16.) The explanation is probably that the frequency of contact is determined in work organizations by job and situational requirements.

As far as *direction* of communication is concerned, there is no reason to suppose that the size of a group, *per se,* would determine the proportion of choices directed upwards, sideways, or downwards. Stratification would be more relevant to this. In fact, the rank order correlations for the eleven groups between group size and the percentage of interaction nominations or influence nominations given to those at the same level, at higher levels, or at lower levels are all close to zero. It is clear that we can look at the relationship between lateral and vertical nominations and structural variables without being worried by the mediating effect of group size.[9]

5 Hierarchical level of group and nominations upwards, downwards, and to peers

One way of examining the effect of different group levels is to compare the supervisory groups (CS1, CS2, CS3, AS1, AS2, and BS) with the middle and top management groups (that is, CM, AM, BM, AT and BT).

Table 6.5
Comparison of managerial and supervisory groups in the three organizations on interaction and influence nominations

	Mean for 5 managerial groups	Mean for 6 supervisory groups	Mann-Whitney U value	p
% of INTERACTION nominations given to people at:				
higher levels	14	22	9	0·165
same level	23	29	9	0·165
lower levels	63	49	4	0·026
% of INFLUENCE nominations given to people at:				
higher levels	33	49	2	0·009
same level	31	21	8	0·123
lower levels	36	30	5	0·041
Mean weekly intra-group interaction frequency:	26	56	10	0·214

A suitable test to use is a non-parametric test, the Mann-Whitney U-test.[10] The figures in Table 6.5 indicate that managerial groups give a greater percentage of interaction nominations to people lower in the organizational hierarchy, and supervisors name a greater percentage of people above them as people to whom they would go for advice. The data in the table also suggest that managerial groups are *influenced* by more people lower in the organization. Mean weekly individual intra-group interaction frequency is similar for managerial and for supervisory groups, i.e. the differences between the means are chance ones.

The differences in downwards and upwards nominations that occur between groups at different levels are consistent with the implications of a hierarchical system itself. People at the top of the hierarchy have more interactions with people below them, but then, there *are* more people below them, and part of the manager's job is to give help and advice to his subordinates. Similarly, it is not surprising that foremen tend to turn to people above them for advice about work matters.

6 The total line management hierarchy and nominations upwards and downwards

A taller hierarchy could increase the possibility for vertical interaction and influence processes. This possibility can be examined by contrasting Aston with Carrs and Brum, for Aston's hierarchy is flatter. The figures for percentage nominations to persons of higher and lower levels are given in Table 6.6, rows 2 and 6. It can be seen that there are no real differences

Table 6.6

Sociometric indices for the groups in the three organizations

	Carrs				Aston				Brum		
	CM	CS1	CS2	CS3	AT	AM	AS1	AS2	BT	BM	BS
Interaction											
1 total nominations	65	90	45	157	89	65	24	95	54	82	66
2 % to people of higher status	12	11	15	28	13	14	25	16	11	16	33
3 % to people of same status	28	25	30	23	30	25	33	39	13	22	25
4 % to people of lower status	60	64	55	49	57	61	42	45	76	62	42
Influence											
5 total nominations	23	37	18	50	50	26	13	34	30	39	23
6 % to people of higher status	26	59	39	60	28	40	75	66	33	39	42
7 % to people of same status	39	30	28	20	36	40	8	22	17	22	21
8 % to people of lower status	34	11	33	20	36	20	17	12	50	39	37

in upward nominations from groups in Carrs and Brum than from groups at Aston. At the bottom of the hierarchy, however, Aston supervisors have smaller spans of control than do the supervisors of Carrs and Brum. The likely effect of this is that Aston supervisors would have a lower percentage of interactions, and perhaps influence nominations, with people lower in the organization. Row 4 in Table 6.6 does not support such an argument for *interaction* nominations. Row 8, on the other hand, shows that, with the exception of CS1, all supervisory groups at Carrs and Brum, where the groups are more stratified by level, have a higher percentage of *influence* nominations going to people lower in the organization than do AS, AS1 and AS2, and in two of the groups the percentage is twice as great as in either of the Aston groups. The height of the total hierarchy, therefore, appears to make little difference to the interaction indices, though at the lower end of the hierarchy a greater number of layers and/or wider span of control seems to affect the influence nominations of supervisors.

7 External departments and lateral choices

We now consider the proportion of nonproduction personnel in relation to interaction and influence processes between members of the line management groups and persons of the same status.

Although some of the nonproduction personnel at Aston and Carrs will be clerks, etc., many of them will be specialists and their assistants. These are the ones with whom line managers will have to deal. It could be expected, therefore, that such nonproduction personnel people are largely at the same levels as middle and top line management. The opportunities for horizontal interaction and influence would be greater in Aston and Carrs than in Brum, which has few support personnel. Row 3 of Table 6.6 offers slight evidence for this, as the two Brum groups BT and BM have the lowest percentage of horizontal interactions. The difference in percentage of horizontal influence nominations is even more convincing, being much lower for BT and BM than for CM, AT and AM (see row 7). The existence of more support personnel at upper and middle levels in the organization does seem to affect the lateral influence exerted by them on members of line groups.

8 Bureaucratic structure, line management hierarchy, and sociometric indices

Table 6.7 presents the information for a number of sociometric indices for each production subsystem as a whole, i.e. all the line management from Chief Executive to first level supervisor. The data here are presented in percentage terms for easy interpretation, but the statistical tests were performed on the raw scores, and simple analysis of variance indicated no difference (beyond the 0·05 level of confidence) between the three companies' production subsystems on any of the interaction or influence measures shown in Table 6.7.

The question is, considering the differences in organization structure among the three companies, what differences in interaction and influence processes would be expected? It could be argued that larger size and more mechanistic features (i.e. greater structuring of activities) would reduce the frequency of interaction. This is how the results turned out, with the small, nonmechanistic organization, Brum, having the highest mean rate of individual interactions per week, and the larger of the two mechanistic organizations, Carrs, having the lowest (see row 4). Indeed, this difference between Carrs and Brum is significant at the 6 per cent level of

Table 6.7

Sociometric indices for the line management hierarchy in the three organizations

	Interaction			Influence		
	Carrs	Aston	Brum	Carrs	Aston	Brum
1 Number completing questionnaire	22	20	13	22	20	13
2 Total number of nominations	293	228	153	113	107	64
3 Mean no. of nominations per person	13·3	11·4	11·8	5·1	5·3	5·1
4 Mean weekly individual interaction frequency[a]	36·1	43·3	60·2*			
5 % intra-subsystem, nominations	28·9	38·8	49·3*	37·5	49·5	59·9*
6 % of nominations to people of higher status	15·1	15·3	20·2	52·0	44·5	41·5
7 % of nominations to people of same status	24·7	29·4	17·9	24·8	29·2	16·8
8 % of nominations to people of lower status	53·9	52·6	54·8	20·6	23·7	40·0
9 Mean no. of nominations for interaction outside own department	4·86	3·70	2·31**			

* The difference between Carrs and Brum is significant ($p < ·05$).
** The difference between Carrs and Brum is significant ($p < ·01$).

[a] The index of interaction frequency was calculated by taking the average of the perceptions of the receiver and the sender: if X says he sees Y 2 p.w. and Y says X 1 p.w., the score given is 1·5 p.w. The correlation between the frequency of mentions given and mentions received was 0·61.

confidence. It must be remembered, however, that across the three companies the differences are not significant, which suggests that despite considerable differences in structure there are wide differences in the frequency of interaction among all these companies. Results from a larger sample of organizations might show more clearly the trend for less mechanistic organizations to have a higher rate of interaction.

We shall now examine in turn the structural differences from the point of view of their theoretical relationship with the interaction and influence indices shown in Table 6.7. The structure scores are those given in the Appendix (*viz*: structuring of activities; centralization of authority; percentage of nonworkflow personnel; hierarchy, and supervisor to worker ratio).

(a) *Mechanistic structuring of work activities*

The structuring of work activities of the mechanistic form of organization could be expected to lead to reduced lateral interaction. It is evident, however, from the percentage nominations to people of the same status shown in Table 6.7, row 7, that it is the nonbureaucracy, Brum, which has the lowest level of lateral interaction, and the lowest level of lateral influence nominations. An explanation of this unexpected finding is to hand, and it is a good example of how the implied effect of one structural component can be altered by the mediation of other structural components. Brum, for a small nonbureaucracy, has an exceptionally tall hierarchy. This increases the possibility for vertical interaction and influence. Brum has eight hierarchical levels, whereas Aston has only five. Carrs also has eight levels (though our study covered only four of them, as shown in Figure 6.1). But Carrs has more opportunity for lateral interactions and influence nominations than Brum. Both Carrs and Aston have many more support (nonproduction) personnel (see Appendix) and, therefore, there are more people at the same level with whom to interact. In other words, in both examples, hierarchy and support personnel, the potential for horizontal interaction and influence was lower in Brum, and this accounts for this finding.

(b) *Centralization of authority*

Brum's greater decentralization might be hypothesized to lead to greater participation, and hence to greater intra-subsystem interaction and influence nominations. Table 6.7 (row 5) shows that Brum does score highest on per cent intra-subsystem nominations, and that the rank ordering of the three companies on this index for both interaction and influence is perfectly in line with the hypothesis, but, again, the differences do not reach an acceptable level of statistical significance across the three companies: the differences between Carrs and Brum alone, however, are significant for both interaction and influence nominations ($p < 0.05$). The figures for interaction with subordinates are also consonant with the decentralized organization having most downwards nominations, though this, too, could be a chance finding, and the complications referred to in connection with structuring of activities are also relevant as mediating explanations here.

(c) *Percentage of non-production personnel*

This feature of organization structure has already been referred to as a variable which has mediated the effects of structuring of activities and concentration of authority. We now consider per cent nonproduction personnel in relation to interaction and influence processes between members of the line management subsystem and outsiders. It will be recalled that the instructions to respondents specifically asked them to carry out the procedure, first for persons within their own department, then separately for persons outside their department, prior to amalgamating the two lists. As Carrs and Aston had more support personnel (see Appendix), we hypothesized that they would have more interaction nominations to other departments than Brum would have. The mean number of nominations for interaction outside the department for Carrs, Aston and Brum, is, respectively, 4·86, 3·70 and 2·31. The difference between Carrs and Brum is significant (p is less than 0·01), but the difference between Aston and Brum is not significant. These findings must be treated with some caution since they hinge on the interpretation placed by respondents on the phrase 'in your own department'.

(d) *Hierarchy*

It was hypothesized that a taller hierarchy would increase the possibility for vertical interaction and influence processes. The figures for percentage nominations to persons of higher and lower levels are given in Table 6.7, rows 6 and 8. The absolute differences are in the expected directions. Carrs and Brum, which each have eight hierarchical levels, have less horizontal interaction, and slightly more upwards and downwards interaction nominations than Aston. The relative differences are, however, not significant.

(e) *Worker to supervisor ratio*

There seems to be no real reason why the fact that Brum and Carrs have fewer supervisors in proportion to production workers should affect their line management subsystems *in toto*. (When discussing the effect of stratification at the *bottom* of the hierarchy it was shown that Carrs and Brum supervisory groups did tend to make more downwards *influence* nominations.)

9 Summary and conclusions

The overall conclusion to be drawn from section 8 and other parts of the chapter is that the processes occurring in organizations result from a complex of effects arising from various features of the organization structure. Generalizations about the effects of bureaucratic structures on behaviour can be seen to be grossly inadequate. Factors such as job level, ratio of workers to supervisors, ratio of staff to direct workers, and degree of stratification, are all factors which may considerably modify the effects of those aspects of bureaucratization which are defined by Pugh et al. (1968) as structuring of activities and concentration of authority. It seems unfortunately true that complex problems require complex solutions.

Relation to some other sociometric studies

One obvious gap in the present study is that we have failed to take account of spatial propinquity. Although there were differences between the three companies with Aston being much more compact than either of the other two organizations, we feel that such factors are unlikely to affect very strongly groups which have existed for a considerable period of time. And, as Simon (1962) says, 'To the extent that interactions are channelled through specialized communications and transportation systems, spatial propinquity becomes less determinitive of structure (i.e., the communication structure, not the formal organization structure).'

When Landsberger (1961) refers to the fact that the frequency and amount of horizontal interactions stem from organizational problems which are themselves rooted in reality problems, he seems to be suggesting, as we have, that the effects of structural components are likely to be swamped by the demands of the real, phenomenological problems experienced by the occupants of the social system. In Berrien's (1967) terms, interactions are responses triggered by input signals from the environment. Nevertheless, the structure may make for differences in the entry points and routing of different types of signals. The interaction and influence differences which do occur as a result of such differences in routing, however, are relatively subtle and not very effectively detected by the rather gross indices used in this study.

Burns (1954) illustrates the relevance of lateral interactions and lateral relationships to the functioning of the vertical hierarchy, even though he thought that its importance, in the case he studied, was 'largely owing to displacement of line communication of status determinants of interaction'. In Carrs, Aston and Brum, interaction at the same level was roughly equivalent to upward interaction. The major differences among the companies were in terms of whether the lateral interaction was intra-group or extra-group, the possibilities for the latter being much greater in the two bureaucracies.

Vertical interaction has also received attention from other writers. Berkowitz and Bennis (1961) studied interaction within and across levels in a hospital. They concluded that nurses initiated more contacts with subordinates than with superiors. In our study, about twice as many persons were mentioned at lower levels than at higher levels. Lower levels accounted for slightly more persons than higher and the same levels combined.

On the other hand, influence choices (as opposed to interaction nominations) are almost always directed upwards. This accords with Berkowitz and Bennis's (1961) findings that the importance of, and satisfaction with, interactions are positively related to the status of the other party.

This review of other sociometric studies looks pathetically small and, even though we have undoubtedly missed some sociometric studies in organizations, there are obviously very few. The study by Allen and Cohen (1969) is an exception. Porter and Lawler (1965), in their review of 'Properties of Organization Structure in Relation to Job Attitudes and Job Behaviour', quote only five studies of interaction/communication in organizations, and none of these was comparative. As we know to our cost, the effort involved and difficulties of handling the enormous complexity of data are not to be undertaken lightly.

In summary, we have shown at various points: (a) that our results are in the predicted direction and that larger studies might confirm real differences, though the relationships are unlikely to be very large, otherwise our design, which uses contrasted extremes, would probably have detected them; and (b) that often the effects of one component of organization structure can be modified or moderated by the effects of another. As Guetzkow, in his review of Communications in Organizations (1965), asks, 'Do we find in communications in organizations an area of study in which there is special richness in contingent, interactive effects?' It would seem that we do, and only a real abundance of insightful, empirical studies is likely to discover just what they are!

Notes

[1] Mechanistic, following Burns and Stalker (1961), is used as a form of shorthand. The Pugh et al. measures used were 'Structuring of Activities' and 'Concentration of Authority'. The more mechanistic organizations had higher scores on both these scales, as shown in the Appendix.

[2] Fuller details are given in Pheysey and Payne (1970).

[3] In Carrs, we were only able to collect information from 22 line managers and supervisory personnel. In Aston, 47 persons completed

questionnaires, of whom 20 were in the line management system described in this paper. In Brum, 14 persons completed questionnaires, of whom 13 were in the line management system described here.

[4]   This is the procedure recommended by Stogdill (1951).

[5]   We also asked a question about liking: 'Please write down the names of those people with whom you would most like to work if you could choose anybody in the organization. Rank them in order of your choice, starting with the person you would most like to work with.' Over twenty-five per cent of the respondents felt unable to respond. Those who did reply tended to use the same names as they had used in answer to the influence question, so we felt that this question had been interpreted more in 'instrumental' terms than in 'attractional' terms.

[6]   Although quite sophisticated methods have been used to identify groups, these methods rest on assumptions which are not valid in our circumstances. Katz (1953), for example, was working with a closed system which would mean that one needed to obtain choices from all the members. Hubbell (1965) does allow for an open system, but he assumes that a person who gives a large number of nominations will be less influenced by (and transfer less influence to) any one of these nominees. In an industrial organization where the criterion is instrumental contacts, it is not possible to say, *a priori,* that the more numerous the choices, the less the importance of any particular choice. We, therefore, decided to use very simple methods.

[7]   One explanation for the fact that less than 100 per cent of the members of these groups spontaneously mentioned the group is that these particular groups were not necessarily the most salient from the point of view of a respondent. In each company, the groups discussed in this paper formed only a quarter or less of the total number of *different* groups which were mentioned by respondents. (Carrs 16 groups, Aston 19 groups, and Brum 16 groups.)

[8]   We provided space for eighteen nominations, and some persons attached additional names on extra paper because they found our provision insufficient! The range and average number of interaction mentions in each of the three companies were:

	Carrs	Aston	Brum
Mean number of mentions			
Per respondent	14	13	12
Range	7–20	5–17	4–22

The average number of nominees given in this open choice situation is close to the average of twelve found by Weiss and Jacobson (1955). They had 2,400 relationships mentioned by 196 respondents. It is relatively unusual to allow people so many choices in sociometric studies, and, as Moreno and Jennings (1938) have pointed out, the extra choices usually confirm the 'stars' in the sociometric pattern, and so, in some ways, do not add very much to our understanding. Our results confirm the first part of this observation, but it is also worth noting that the average frequency of interaction with the nominee ranked thirteenth across the three companies, is still 4·4 times per week ($N = 29$), or almost one per day. Had we considered even the first four nominations only, we would have excluded many interactions of importance, and concluded that almost no intra-group interaction occurs in these formally defined groups, other than interaction with the official leader.

[9] Size accounts for much of the variance in *intra-group* interaction and influence *nominations;* however, with only eleven groups and three organizations it would be very difficult to account for the remainder. Had we a larger sample, partial correlations would help.

If we wish to account separately for the mediating effect of job level, for example, on the relationship between other structural variables and interaction and influence, we must either partial out for group size or ensure that group size is unrelated to job level. Although the eleven groups cover but three levels, the rank order correlation between level and group size, correcting for ties, is only 0·14 (n.s.).

[10] This test can also be used to ascertain whether or not differences in the size of the managerial versus supervisory groups are sufficiently large as to affect the other relationships in which we are interested. The supervisory groups do not differ in size from the managerial groups ($U = 13, p = 0·396$), so we can discount size effects between the levels.

Appendix
Positions of the three manufacturing companies on key organization variables

	Carrs	Aston	Brum
1 Number of employees	2,912	350	412
2 Woodward technology category	mass	small batch	small batch
3 Structuring of activities	62	57	35
4 Concentration of authority (i.e. centralization at higher levels)	50	47	27
5 % nonproduction personnel	52	52	26
6 Number of levels in hierarchy	8	5	8
7 Workers per supervisor	43	12	38

Scores on variables 3 and 4 are standard scores, having a mean of 50 and a standard deviation of 15, based on the original sample of 52 Midlands organizations.

PART III
CLIMATE STUDIES

7 Stern's organizational climate index: a reconceptualization and application to business organizations*

R.L. PAYNE and D.C. PHEYSEY

G.G. Stern and his one-time colleague C.R. Pace are two of the few social scientists who have concerned themselves with the conceptualization and measurement of dimensions of the environment, albeit in this case the perceived environment. As the behaviour of any biological or social system is a function of the interaction between the system and its environment this kind of work would seem a crucial step if we are to improve our ability to predict the behaviour of such systems.

It is, perhaps, not surprising that psychologists should turn first of all to a psychological framework within which to conceptualize the environment. Pursuing the idea expressed by G.G. Stern, M.I. Stein and B.S. Bloom (1956), the above-mentioned researchers developed a measure of the college environment (CCI – the College Characteristics Index) by constructing 30 environmental press scales which were assumed to be counterparts of the 30 personality need scales which Stern had taken from H.A. Murray (1938) to construct a personality measure, the Activities Index (Stern et al., 1956). The possibilities offered by having a personality and an environmental measure of the same concepts are considerable, and Stern (1967) reported an extensive body of interesting work using both instruments. In the same report he included other instruments developed from the CCI, namely High School and Evening College Characteristics Indexes, and a more general Organizational Climate Index (OCI). C.R. Pace (1963), however, became less concerned with the interaction between the individual personality and its perception of the environmental presses to which it was submitted, and developed an interest in the nature of the

---

* originally published in *Organizational Behaviour and Human Performance*, vol. 6, 1971, pp. 77–98.

educational institution *per se,* which led to the construction of an instrument called CUES, the College and University Environment Scales. Pace, too, reports a range of interesting results using his instrument (Pace, 1966).

The present writers' interests in the perception of the environment arose from a different quarter. We were, and are, involved in a research programme concerned with the structure and functioning of organizations as outlined by Pugh et al. (1963). The first part of the research programme involved the measurement of organization context and structure and appears in Pugh et al. (1968, 1969). Thus, we arrived at an interest in the perception of organizational environment, not from the standpoint of the individual's psychological views, but from the standpoint of the relationship between the perception of the environment and more objective measures of the organization's structure, which, as we have suggested elsewhere (Inkson et al., 1967), can also be conceptualized as environmental dimensions. It is not surprising, therefore, that in considering the measurement of the organizational environment we were most concerned to construct scales around those concepts common to the structure and functioning of work organizations, rather than the structure and functioning of individual personalities. However, the OCI seemed such a rich source of items about organizations that we decided to try and use the same items, but to reconceptualize them according to what we considered more appropriate concepts. The measure in its amended form we shall call the Business Oganization Climate Index, or BOCI.

The procedure

The 300 items from the OCI were typed on separate pieces of paper and then the writers sorted them into groups of items which seemed to have a common meaning or interest. By successive sortings we eventually arrived at six broad groupings - authority, restraint, work interest, personal relations, routine or control, wider community - and 46 residual items which we discarded as inappropriate to business organizations, or to a British population. We then sorted each of the six subcategories again according to their common meaning or interest. By this procedure we sorted 254 items into 24 different conceptual areas. The 24 groupings were then named in accordance with their apparent meaning as concepts which would 'fit' the business organization, for example, administrative efficiency, rules orientation, scientific and technical orientation, etc. The BOCI questionnaire was then constructed in which each item was to be scored 'true' or 'false', and it was administered to 120 junior/middle managers from more than 100 different companies. The respondents were all attending full-time or part-time management education courses in three different institutions: an industry staff college, a college of technology, and a university.

The results

The scales were subjected to item analysis, using the Brogden-Clemens coefficient, a variation of the biserial correlation coefficient, to calculate the correlation of each item with the total scale score. This coefficient is particularly useful for item analysis for it has the interesting properties of (a) not penalizing items which have difficulty levels removed from a 50–50 split and (b) not making the bivariate normality assumption (see Levy and Pugh, 1969). Due to these properties items were rejected only if less than 10 per cent or more than 90 per cent of people responded positively to the item, and/or if the correlation of the item with the total was low. The coefficients have not been corrected to allow for the necessary correlation between the item and the total which arises from the item's contribution to the total score, and this can be quite substantial in short scales, but items have been rejected if they do not have a correlation considerably greater than $1/\sqrt{n}$, where n = number of items in the scale.

Table 7.1 contains the titles of the 24 scales, the number of items in each scale, and their original mean correlation values, plus the number of items in the revised scales (that is, after poor items have been rejected) and their mean correlation values. The table also includes split-half reliability coefficients using Flanagan's formula (Guildford, 1954). As this formula gives the reliability for the total score it is not necessary to use the Spearman-Brown correction. Except for the shortness of the scales physical caution, homogeneity, and variety in physical environment, the scales seem to have reasonable item-analysis values, coupled with satisfactory reliability for such short scales. The only exceptions as far as reliability is concerned are the scales of homogeneity, intellectual orientation, and physical caution. The Appendix contains examples of typical items in each of the 24 scales, and the mean and standard deviation for each scale.

In addition to using the split-half method of estimating reliability, we have been able to use the test-retest method on a small sample of

Table 7.1
Item analysis values for original and reduced scales in BOCI

Scale title	Original number of items	Mean general bi-serial cor-relation	Reduced number of items	Mean general bi-serial cor-relation	Split-half reliability
Authority scales					
Leaders' psychological distance	12	0·63	8	0·68	0·64
Questioning authority	9	0·75	7	0·77	0·76
Egalitarianism	6	0·77	6	0·77	0·82
Management concern for employee involvement	10	0·76	10	0·76	0·88
Restraint scales					
Open-mindedness	10	0·74	8	0·74	0·82
Emotional control	11	0·60	7	0·71	0·64
Physical caution	5	0·72	4	0·81	0·58
Work interest scales					
Practical orientation	10	0·64	6	0·75	0·72
Future orientation	7	0·82	6	0·83	0·86
Scientific and technical orientation	8	0·72	8	0·72	0·88
Intellectual orientation	11	0·73	11	0·73	0·46
Job challenge	11	0·65	11	0·65	0·66
Task orientation	9	0·75	8	0·77	0·84
Industriousness	20	0·74	14	0·75	0·86
Personal relations scales					
Altruism	7	0·69	7	0·69	0·62
Sociability	18	0·71	10	0·75	0·92
Interpersonal aggression	10	0·71	6	0·76	0·78
Homogeneity	5	0·65	4	0·68	0·26
Routine scales					
Rules orientation	8	0·68	6	0·73	0·72
Administrative efficiency	20	0·67	9	0·75	0·78
Conventionality	14	0·69	10	0·71	0·82
Readiness to innovate	10	0·71	9	0·72	0·80
Variety in physical environment	7	0·73	5	0·77	0·60
Community scales					
Orientation to wider community	16	0·65	12	0·66	0·72
Total	254		192		

supervisors in a motor vehicle assembly shop. The two administrations of the instrument were separated by a period of seven weeks. In the first administration 17 supervisors completed the BOCI and in the second 11 supervisors (drawn from the initial 17). As we had promised complete anonymity in this study, we did not even use code numbers and, therefore, had to use analysis of variance rather than correlation to test reliability. We found that the scale of scientific and technical orientation is the only one where there is a significant difference between the two occasions at the 5 per cent level of confidence. Only five of the scales have an F ratio much greater than 1·0. The five are emotional control (3·03), intellectual orientation (2·47), job challenge (3·55), conventionality (2·90), and variety in physical environment (2·77). The fact that for 18 of the scales the F ratio is so low supports the reliability of the instrument.

At this point it seemed of interest to ask whether our scales were as good as Stern's version. We, therefore, scored our 120 respondents on as many of Stern's scales as we could. As we had excluded 46 items from the questionnaire, we did not have sufficient items to score 3 of the 30 scales: humanities and social sciences, sexuality, and reflectiveness. Several other scales were shortened from Stern's 10 items per scale to as few as six in the case of one scale. Table 7.2 shows the number of items in each of the remaining 27 scales, the scale titles, and the mean general biserial correlation coefficient for the original scales and the improved version, from which the poorer items in the scale have been removed (see table footnote). The comments in brackets after the scale titles indicate our interpretation of what some of the scales measure – some of the need press concepts are, to us, quite misleading. As a comparison of Tables 7.1 and 7.2 indicates, our scales have slightly higher mean correlation coefficients. In fact, the mean of the mean correlation coefficients for the Stern scales is 0·64 and for our scales 0·74.

Having established the basic psychometric properties of our scales it is of interest to know the degree to which they are similar to or different from those of Stern. The correlations of the two sets of scales are available on application to the writers. As one would expect, there are many high positive correlations. In four cases one of Stern's scales correlates over 0·90 with one of the BOCI scales. The four instances are scientific orientation with scientism, physical caution with harm avoidance, conventionality with narcissism, and industriousness with energy. As these scales have a high percentage of common items, they are clearly measuring something similar. Overall, however, there are only 24 correlations which are over 0·71 out of a total of 648 correlation coefficients; in other words, there are only 24 instances (spread over 16 of

Table 7.2
Item analysis of Stern's scales on Birmingham sample

	Number of items	Average general bi-serial corre-lation	Reduced number of items	Revised general bi-serial corre-lation[a]
Assurance/abasement	10	0·61	9	0·62
Achievement	10	0·68	8	0·70
Adaptiveness (acceptance of supervision)	9	0·61	6	0·64
Affiliation/rejection	10	0·73	8	0·75
Blame avoidance/aggression	9	0·51	7	0·53
Change/sameness	10	0·55	9	0·56
Conjunctivity (planning)	10	0·75	9	0·76
Counteraction	10	0·51	9	0·52
Deference	9	0·51	7	0·53
Dominance	8	0·63	6	0·65
Ego achievement	6	0·67	6	0·67
Placidity/emotionality	10	0·52	6	0·56
Energy/passivity	9	0·71	8	0·72
Exhibitionism	9	0·60	6	0·63
Fantasied achievement	8	0·65	7	0·66
Harm avoidance	8	0·62	6	0·64
Impulsion/deliberation	10	0·57	8	0·59
Narcissism (conformity)	10	0·68	8	0·70
Nurturance/rejection	9	0·63	6	0·66
Objectivity	9	0·70	8	0·71
Order	10	0·57	6	0·61
Work/play	9	0·58	6	0·61
Pragmatism (practicalness)	9	0·46	6	0·49
Scientism	8	0·79	8	0·79
Sentience	6	0·61	6	0·61
Succourance/autonomy	9	0·61	6	0·64
Understanding[b]	8	0·73	8	0·73
Total	242		193	

[a] As we were not primarily interested in Stern's scales we did not attempt to re-item analyze his scales. However, on the basis of our own data we found an average improvement in the mean item analysis value of 0·01 per item removed. This column allows an improvement of 0·01 per item removed as a rough measure of the values for the improved scales.

[b] Because we believed the items were inappropriate, either for our purposes, or for use with a British population, we excluded 46 items from Stern's OCI. As a result these three scales did not have sufficient items in our version: humanities and social science; sexuality; reflectiveness.

our 24 scales) where there is more than 50 per cent common variance between two scales. In these 16 scales we are measuring a similar concept to Stern's, but our measure is generally slightly better. For example, the mean item-analysis values for BOCI emotional control = 0·71, but the OCI value for emotionality = 0·56; BOCI has 0·74 for open-mindedness and Stern 0·71 for objectivity, etc. In the other cases we are measuring something different from Stern's scales, for example, our variety in the physical environment. The main difference, however, is that we have conceptualized the scales in terms of concepts which are familiar in the management situation, which makes them more readily comparable to other concepts in the literature of organization theory, such as bureaucracy (rules orientation and administrative efficiency), production centredness (task-orientation and industriousness) and employee-centredness (sociability, leaders' psychological distance, management concern for employee involvement).

The use of individual perceptions to characterize organizations

Both the OCI and BOCI measures use the aggregate score of individuals to represent the larger system. It is, therefore, important to know whether the measure of central tendency used really does reflect fairly the views of the aggregate population as a whole or whether there are sizeable differences between the average scores of subcategories of the total system. We tested this out in two companies, Aston and Brum, by comparing the mean score of the group of executives responsible for policy-making with the score of respondents in the other managerial groups we studied in each organization (see Pheysey, Payne and Pugh, 1970, for complete details). This meant that there were six managers in the top executive group at Aston and 13 managers in lower groups, and five managers in the top executive groups at Brum with nine managers in other groups. Using simple analysis of variance to compare the top groups with the rest of the managers in each organization we found only 1 instance out of 48 where there was a difference between the top managers and the rest. This difference occurred in Aston where the top management saw the organization as being significantly lower on administrative efficiency (p < 0·05). In these two organizations at least, top and middle management seem to agree very well about the nature of the organizational climate in which they work. We also separated out the 19 line management from the 31 specialist staff at Aston and again found that analysis of variance revealed no significant differences between them. There were few staff personnel at Brum, so we did not perform a similar

Table 7.3
Principal-components analysis of the 24 BOCI scales[a]

	Factor					
	I	II	III	IV	V	h²
Authority scales						
Leaders' psychological distance	—54	54	28	00	—20	70
Questioning authority	67	—39	21	—22	—01	69
Egalitarianism	40	—22	—33	46	—13	55
Management concern for employee involvement	80	—20	—21	—16	19	78
Restraint scales						
Open-mindedness	74	—48	—13	—17	—02	82
Emotional control	—33	48	—11	52	30	71
Physical caution	54	46	—16	—45	01	73
Work interest scales						
Practical orientation	72	04	—09	12	22	59
Future orientation	82	11	—06	08	01	69
Scientific and technical orientation	77	18	—07	01	22	68
Intellectual orientation	83	—02	14	03	19	75
Job challenge	79	07	32	05	01	73
Task orientation	75	07	16	20	—28	71
Industriousness	69	—09	14	37	—32	74
Personal relations scales						
Altruism	65	—06	—15	—06	34	57
Sociability	68	14	08	—16	—04	52
Interpersonal aggression	—53	37	35	—14	—24	62
Homogeneity	—22	00	—73	—09	38	73
Routine scales						
Rules orientation	42	56	—21	—25	—23	65
Administrative efficiency	64	28	—16	03	—26	58
Conventionality	30	59	—11	26	16	54
Readiness to innovate	26	16	50	13	—28	44
Variety in physical environment	59	30	—06	17	20	51
Community scales						
Orientation to wider community	73	41	04	—27	06	78
% variance	36·3	9·3	5·7	5·3	4·5	

[a] Decimal points have been omitted.

split there. It would thus seem a valid procedure to take the mean score of the individuals in the organization as an indicator of the general climate in the organization, at least at the management level. Ultimately, the correct procedure would be to take a representative sample of shop-floor workers, too, in order to see whether there were significant differences between them and management personnel.

Factor analysis of BOCI and OCI

In an attempt to simplify the wealth of data, the 24 BOCI scales were intercorrelated, and a principal-components analysis performed on the matrix. Table 7.3 shows the results of this analysis. The correlation matrix is available on request to the writers.

Although the first five factors had roots greater than 1·0, only the first two seem to have conceptual meaning. As so often occurs with the principal-components method, the first factor is almost a general factor, a large proportion of the scales having high factor loadings on it. The factor has been called 'Organizational progressiveness'. The 10 scales having the highest loadings on the factor were entered into a multiple regression on to the factor in order to calculate factor scores. Five scales had a multiple correlation of 0·97 with the factor. The five scales are intellectual orientation ($\beta = 0.17$), future orientation ($\beta = 0.23$), management concern for employee involvement ($\beta = 0.34$), scientific and technical orientation ($\beta = 0.18$), and task orientation ($\beta = 0.25$). In calculating factor scores, all these five scales, except for management concern for employee involvement, were given robust weightings of 1·0, the last-named scale was given a weighting of 2·0. These weightings were applied for an empirical reason (the weightings themselves) and for a conceptual reason. Management concern for employee involvement indicates a progressive attitude to personal and interpersonal needs, while the other four scales reflect progressive attitudes towards problems concerned with the central task of the organization. This distinction between the task and social aspects of social collectivities has consistently appeared in factor analyses of smaller social collectivities (see Stogdill, 1959, for a review of these studies) and it, therefore, seems empirically and conceptually appropriate that they contribute a fairly balanced weighting to a factor describing a larger social collectivity – scales concerned with task aspects still contribute twice as much as the social aspects in fact.

The second factor has been named 'normative control'. Four scales have high loadings on this factor, and they have a multiple correlation of 0·91 with the factor. The scales are conventionality ($\beta = 0.35$), leaders' psychological distance (β = 0·40), rules orientation (β = 0·42), and emotional control (β = 0·33). Each scale was given a robust weighting of 1·0 when calculating factor scores.

As Table 7.3 shows, Factor III has a high negative loading on the scale homogeneity, but, as we have already shown, this is a short and unreliable scale and we do not regard Factor III as having an unambiguous psychological or sociological meaning. Factors IV and V similarly do not have any immediately obvious connotation.

The first two factors were plotted graphically against each other and inspected for possible orthogonal rotation. Rotation did not improve the meaning of the factors, however, and the original solution was accepted as the best.

The two factors produced by the principal-components analysis of our data are very similar to two second-order factors produced by Stern's analysis of the OCI. Stern (1967) called his first second-order factor 'development press'. The primary factors which were loaded on this were personal dignity, intellectual climate, achievement standards, and group life. It can be seen that these cover both task and socioemotional aspects as did the scales in our own factor of organizational progressiveness. Stern called his second second-order factor 'control press'. The primary factors having the highest loading on this factor were orderliness and impulse control, which are obviously very similar to our scales of conventionality and rules orientation, and emotional control, respectively.

When our data were factor analyzed with the scales scored according to Stern's concepts the same two factors appeared. Six factors have roots above 1·0. Factors I and II are clearly development and control press factors, respectively. The highest loadings on Factor I are the scales of achievement, scientism, objectivity, understanding, and succourance; and the highest loadings on Factor II are order, narcissism (which is really concerned with the stress on social conformity), and deference.

Factor III is not unlike Factor II in meaning. Its three major scales are dominance (lack of), blame avoidance, and work, and it would seem to represent a dimension of submissiveness. Factor IV has loadings on work, energy, change, and two of the achievement scales: it seems to be something like effort press. Factor V has only one sizeable loading and thus may be called practicality press. Factor VI seems to have no particularly obvious meaning.

So far it has been demonstrated that the BOCI reconceptualization of the items in Stern's OCI has resulted in slightly better psychometric scales, and two major factors which are very similar in meaning whichever way the items are conceptualized. However, we believe that for theoretical and practical purposes it is very useful to describe the organizational climate in terms of concepts relating to organization rather than in terms of psychological constructs, though as we detail in the conclusions we do not deny the validity of such an approach. We are, however, in sympathy with Pace (1966) when he commented on the contrast between Stern's CCI and his own measure CUES, '. . . the organization of environments is different in many ways from the organization of personalities' and '. . . the variables which will account for institutional differences in environment will do so more because of their educational content (in our case read business content) than because of their psychological content'. We conclude with a description of a field study using the BOCI, which, as well as demonstrating its usefulness, provides some evidence for the construct validity of the scales and factors.

A field study using the BOCI

The main purpose of the study from which the following description is extracted was to examine the relationship between organization structure and the structure and functioning of managerial groups within the organization. This study is described in full in Chapter 5. What is relevant here is that two organizations were studied and that these were very carefully selected so that they were very similar on important aspects of organizational context, but very dissimilar on aspects of organizational structure (Pugh et al., 1963). That is, the organizations were of similar size, and the degree of integration of their operations technology (Hickson et al., 1969) was also very similar – although their products were not the same. In terms of organization structure, however, they were quite different. Aston had many rules, regulations and standard procedures and had a more centralized authority structure, whereas Brum had very few rules, regulations, or standard procedures, and operated a very decentralized authority structure. Detailed comparisons are presented in the Appendix to Chapter 6.

Table 7.4 presents means, standard deviations, and F ratio for simple analysis of variance between the scores of the two companies on the BOCI scales, and the two factors. Scores of the 120 subjects in the original study were used as a basis for standardization. Component scales of factors were converted to standard scores having a mean of 100 and standard deviation of 10. The factor scores themselves were then standardized to the same mean and standard deviation. There were 50 respondents in Aston, all of whom were supervisors or managers, or in technical positions of equivalent status. There were 22 respondents from Brum who also held supervisory, managerial, or technical posts.

Table 7.4
Analysis of variance between Aston and Brum BOCI

	Aston (50)		Brum (22)		
	Mean	*SD*	Mean	*SD*	*F* ratio
Authority scales					
Leaders' psychological distance	1·76	1·20	2·58	1·50	8·58**
Questioning authority	4·59	1·73	3·52	2·22	5·36*
Egalitarianism	4·18	1·87	3·42	2·14	0·79
Management concern for employee involvement	8·51	1·94	7·89	2·23	2·46
Restraint scales					
Open-mindedness	5·65	2·15	4·68	2·45	3·44
Emotional control	3·88	1·68	3·47	1·50	0·26
Physical caution	3·55	0·61	3·10	0·99	5·20*
Work interest scales					
Practical orientation	5·40	0·96	4·42	1·74	11·92**
Future orientation	4·84	1·14	3·68	1·91	13·36**
Scientific and technical orientation	5·74	1·68	3·68	2·40	18·73**
Intellectual orientation	7·06	1·72	5·00	2·79	16·08**
Job challenge	7·38	1·97	5·63	2·67	10·73**
Task orientation	5·72	1·84	4·47	2·39	8·39**
Industriousness	10·42	2·82	5·84	4·10	31·55**
Personal relations scales					
Altruism	3·92	1·84	5·11	1·66	7·60**
Sociability	5·84	2·31	5·58	3·08	0·28
Interpersonal aggression	1·71	1·76	1·84	1·80	0·16
Homogeneity	1·41	0·99	1·11	0·94	0·71
Routine scales					
Rules orientation	5·41	0·79	4·52	1·39	13·55**
Administrative efficiency	6·67	2·07	4·00	2·91	20·59**
Conventionality	7·37	1·52	5·63	1·92	16·35**
Readiness to innovate	5·02	1·66	3·89	1·97	9·91**
Variety in physical environment	2·61	0·93	2·16	1·12	2·98
Community scales					
Orientation to wider community	5·40	2·41	7·37	3·23	9·53**
Factors					
1 Organizational progressiveness	108·42	6·30	101·45	9·70	12·74**
2 Normative control	103·24	6·90	100·86	7·84	1·61

* $p < ·05$ ** $p < ·01$

As a result of the structural differences we hypothesized differences in the climate as perceived by the employees. Due to its rules, regulations, and standard procedures, Aston would be expected to have a climate more concerned with rules orientation–administrative efficiency and as a result to be more concerned with being conventional. As Table 7.4 shows, Aston is significantly different from Brum in all these respects. An intellectual approach to the design of the administrative system is unlikely to be limited to such problems, but is almost sure to be applied to the work system too. This seems true of Aston, as is reflected by their significantly higher scores on all the work interest scales. The differences on these scales cause the difference between the two companies on Factor I, organizational progressiveness: on the other major scale in the factor, management concern for employee involvement, Brum scores only slightly lower than Aston. Aston really does seem more progressive, for the scales also reveal that it is more 'ready to innovate' and more ready to 'question authority'.

In view of the fact that decision-taking authority in Aston is very centralized compared to Brum, it is perhaps surprising that Aston does score higher on questioning authority. One of the effects of decentralization in Brum, however, is to give more power to the people who are closer to those who operate the instructions. This is reflected in the greater number of hierarchical levels in Brum (eight) compared to Aston (only five). The effect of this is that people lower in the organization use their power, and their subordinates have less opportunity to appeal to a higher authority figure, as the organization invests immediate superordinates with the requisite authority anyway. This really involves the distinction between the aspects of decentralization which are described by Hage and Aiken (1967) as hierarchical decentralization (which the Pugh et al. scales measure) and participation – the number of people who are involved in a decision. Thus, Brum is hierarchically decentralized, but low on participation. We hypothesize that it is for this reason that Brum scores significantly higher on leaders' psychological distance, whereas much of the literature on decentralization would have indicated the reverse relationship. Nevertheless, Brum's score of 2·58 out of a possible score of 8 for leaders' psychological distance indicates that they are distant only relatively to Aston leaders. As the Appendix shows, the mean score on this scale for the original sample of 120 is 3·13.

This difference on leaders' psychological distance is important in the case of these two organizations, for it is largely responsible for the lack of difference between Aston and Brum on Factor II, normative control. Certainly one would hypothesize that Aston would be higher on normative control than Brum. It is not, because leaders' psychological distance is one of the component scales of the factor, and this difference nullifies the effect of the differences where Aston does score higher on the control end of the factor, namely, on the scales of rules orientation and conventionality. Thus Brum may be a relatively unusual organization to have such a pattern of control processes.

The consideration of some data on a third organization further substantiates the construct validity of the BOCI and also illustrates its usefulness in describing an organization's climate. This organization (Carrs) manufactures motor vehicles, and it forms a very useful comparison with Aston because it is very similar on the three main structural variables, structuring of activities, concentration of authority, and percentage of nonproduction personnel. It is also similar to Aston in that it is part of a large group and hence scores high on the contextual scale of dependence and also on the scale measuring the degree of integration of operations technology. The essential difference between the two organizations, however, is that Carrs is more than eight times as large as Aston. In simple terms, we might say we have a small manufacturing bureaucracy and a rather large manufacturing bureaucracy. Structural details are again given in the Appendix to Chapter 6.

It is well known from other work (reviewed by Porter and Lawler, 1965) that size of organization has a deleterious effect on job satisfaction, absence, turnover, etc., and it can be expected, therefore, that a large bureaucracy, particularly one with a high ratio of workers to supervisors and a tall management hierarchy, would find it more difficult to create a climate where people felt that the organization was progressive, that it had control of its affairs and was developing well, and yet where people could feel close to their superiors, and free to use their own initiative. Due to the greater number of people, the large bureaucracy would find it difficult to create such good communications and interpersonal relations, so that the alienating effects of the bureaucratic rules (Gouldner, 1955) could not be countered by the good interpersonal relations which it would be easier to create in a small company. All other things being equal then, because there are more hierarchical levels in Carrs, and because work groups are very large, people working there would tend to feel that leaders were psychologically distant, and hence that management lacks concern for employee involvement, and that the organization is rather unsociable. These generally alienating conditions would reduce commitment to work, resulting in low work interest on the part of both production and administrative staff. These conditions would lead to the prediction that Carrs would be higher on the scale leaders' psychological distance, and

Table 7.5
Analysis of variance between Aston and Carrs BOCI

	Aston (50)		Carrs (21)		
	Mean	*SD*	Mean	*SD*	*F* ratio
Authority scales					
Leaders' psychological distance	1·76	1·20	3·28	2·00	15·10**
Questioning authority	4·59	1·73	4·57	2·01	00·00
Egalitarianism	4·18	1·87	3·76	1·99	00·71
Management concern for employee involvement	8·51	1·94	6·66	2·88	9·58**
Restraint scales					
Open-mindedness	5·65	2·15	4·33	1·81	5·85*
Emotional control	3·38	1·68	3·61	1·55	0·28
Physical caution	3·55	0·61	3·00	0·97	7·96**
Work interest scales					
Practical orientation	5·40	0·96	4·23	1·63	13·78**
Future orientation	4·84	1·14	3·52	1·84	12·92**
Scientific and technical orientation	5·74	1·68	3·57	2·17	19·93**
Intellectual orientation	7·06	1·72	5·33	2·71	10·04**
Job challenge	7·36	1·97	6·52	1·76	2·84
Task orientation	5·72	1·84	4·04	2·73	8·70**
Industriousness	10·42	2·82	8·14	3·68	7·83**
Personal relations scales					
Altruism	3·92	1·84	3·38	2·10	1·13
Sociability	5·84	2·31	4·28	2·62	6·00*
Interpersonal aggression	1·71	1·76	2·57	1·84	3·35
Homogeneity	1·41	0·99	1·33	0·89	0·08
Routine scales					
Rules orientation	5·41	0·79	4·47	1·43	11·93**
Administrative efficiency	6·67	2·07	3·80	2·48	24·55**
Conventionality	7·37	1·52	6·71	2·02	2·16
Readiness to innovate	5·02	1·66	4·09	1·74	4·35*
Variety in physical environment	2·61	0·93	1·38	1·13	22·28**
Community scales					
Orientation to wider community	4·50	2·41	5·33	2·35	0·01
Factors					
1 Organizational progressiveness	108·42	6·30	99·33	11·33	17·89**
2 Normative control	103·24	6·90	103·71	9·76	0·01

* $p < ·05$ **$p < ·01$

lower on management concern for employee involvement, sociability, task-orientation and industriousness, and on such work-related scales as administrative efficiency. As Table 7.5 shows, Carrs does score significantly different from Aston on all these scales. As it happens, Aston has also created a climate which is more open-minded and yet more concerned with rules and efficient administration, while still being very concerned with the intellectual, scientific, and technical aspects of its work. The latter differences cause the significant difference between the two companies on Factor I, organizational progressiveness. As they are both bureaucracies they would not be expected to be different on normative control, and they have almost exactly the same scores on this factor. Because of its small size, Aston seems to have achieved all the benefits of the rationality of the bureaucratic system and few, if any, of the costs. This pattern of scores then further validates the BOCI scales in terms of other work on the effects of organization size, and seems to indicate its usefulness in relating perceptual data to structural aspects of organizations.

The explanation offered in the preceding paragraph certainly makes sense in terms of one's subjective impression of the companies. Aston really is much more progressive; for example, it is part of a large international corporation, has its own R and D function, and has access to all the latest managerial techniques and know-how. It is also performing extremely well. Both Brum and Carrs, on the other hand, are not doing very well and Carrs in particular has been struggling for some time. The danger is that such impressions may have affected the explanations themselves – only further research will answer that criticism. But since BOCI scales are related to structural differences among these companies, and since they do reflect differences which were subjectively perceived by the authors, we feel that they are also reasonably valid measures of the concepts they describe. In addition, as demonstrated earlier, the scales have reasonable psychometric properties. We conclude, therefore, that this reconceptualization of Stern's OCI is a useful tool for the analysis of the perceived climate of business organizations, and that structural analysis needs to be supplemented by measures of climate if we are to understand more fully variations in organizational functioning and performance.

In saying this we are not suggesting that Stern's conceptualization is either wrong or not useful. We would merely point out that Stern was interested in the fit between personality and environment and believed with Lewin that 'we can best maximize this sort of relevance of personality to environment by conceptualizing and measuring these two

Table 7.6
Possible types of data about persons and environment[a]

Conceptualization	Perceptual				Objective	
	Individually perceived		Other perceived			
	Psychological	Environmental	Psychological	Environmental	Psychological	Environmental
Person	Self-ratings, etc., e.g. Stern's Activities Index (1)	Self-ratings of adjustment to environmental stress (2)	Ratings of traits, etc. (3)	Ratings of physical attributes, perceived reactions to environments (4)	Performance tests, etc. (5)	Psychological, sociological measures: behaviours in stress, or different environments (6)
Environment	Perceptions of need presses, e.g. Stern's OCI (7)	Perceptions of climate, and situations in general (8)	Group means as measures of climate, e.g. Stern's OCI (9)	Group means as measures of environment, e.g. BOCI (10)	Counts of aggressive, regressive acts, e.g. aspects of R.G. Barker's 'Behaviour Episodes' (1968) (11)	Sociological measures, physical measures, counts, charts, memos, etc., e.g. R.G. Barker's 'Behaviour Settings' (1968) (12)

[a] The descriptions in the boxes are given only as examples and are not exhaustive of the possible kinds of data that might be collected.

terms in commensurate dimensions . . .' (Lewin, 1951). Accepting this argument, the Need Press Theory of Murray is a convenient framework with which to conceptualize personality dimensions and their concomitant environmental presses, for the individual's perceptions of himself and the environment then becomes the common link between the two concepts. Sells (1963) on the other hand, rejected this argument and insisted that measures of the environment need to be independent of the person's perceptions of them. We do not feel that it is a question of either perceptual data or objective data, but more a question of the utility of both kinds of data in predicting the behaviour either of individuals or environments (particularly organizations as environments) (see also Pervin, 1968). The various possible types of data that can be collected about persons and their environment are presented in Table 7.6.

The table is based on the two assumptions (a) that data about the person and his environment can be acquired from three sources: the person himself, people around about him, and by objective measures (where these are recording of a person's actions, etc., they are often recorded by people, of course – the investigators – but they are objective in the sense of not being based on opinion or interpretation); (b) that the concepts used for systematizing the data about the person and his environment can be framed in psychological or environmental terms.

There seems to us to be no reason for any of these 12 types of data to be regarded as intrinsically superior to any of the others. All 12 types are in themselves interesting and tell us different things about people and their environments. We cannot see any reason why the relationships between all 12 types of data (132 in all) might not be of value. Indeed, it might be very valuable indeed to know the efficiency of prediction when all six types of data about the person are congruent compared with when they are incongruent, or to know under what conditions each of these two situations (congruent and incongruent data) will predict what and how efficiently. Regarded in this light the BOCI scales are type-10 data which have been related to the structural dimensions of organizations which are type-12 data. Stern's CCI was designed to be used in conjunction with the personality measure, the Activities Index, and these are types 1 and 7, respectively, though the CCI can obviously be used as type-9 data.

In summary, we have shown that the BOCI is a psychometrically sound instrument, having a reasonable degree of construct validity, and that it provides one type of data about organizations as an environment that has both theoretical and practical relevance.

Appendix

Examples of items from the 24 BOCI Scales, and means and standard deviations for each scale ($N = 120$)

Scale title	Mean	SD
Authority scales		
Leaders' psychological distance	3·13	1·88
Senior personnel are frequently jealous of their authority		
There is a lot of bootlicking (apple polishing) here		
Questioning authority	3·29	2·21
People avoid direct clashes with senior personnel at all costs		
People who get pushed around here are expected to fight back		
Egalitarianism	3·26	1·82
There are no favourites in this place — everyone gets treated alike		
Management concern for employee involvement	6·38	2·83
There are few opportunities for informal conversation with senior personnel		
Senior personnel will go out of their way to help you with your work		
Restraint scales		
Open-mindedness	4·36	2·46
People here speak out openly		
Criticism is taken as a personal affront in this organization		
Emotional control	3·38	1·97
People here tend to hide their deeper feelings from each other		
Physical caution	2·49	1·29
Everyone here is safety conscious, anxious to avoid accidents and put right the conditions which produce them		
Work interest scales		
Practical orientation	4·05	1·61
The work atmosphere emphasizes efficiency and usefulness		

Scale title	Mean	*SD*
People here are generally efficient and successful in practical affairs		
Future orientation	3·24	1·99
The ability to plan ahead is highly valued here		
People here are encouraged to take a long-term view		
Scientific and technical orientation	4·76	2·46
A discussion about the latest scientific inventions would not be uncommon here		
Intellectual orientation	5·13	3·08
Few people here are stimulated by intellectual activities or problems		
Careful reasoning and clear logic are highly valued here		
Job challenge	5·13	2·59
Most activities present a real personal challenge		
Task orientation	3·70	2·43
People here follow the maxim 'business before pleasure'		
People here feel they must really work hard because of the important nature of their work		
Industriousness	6·50	4·16
It is fairly easy to keep up here without working too hard		
There is so much to do here that people are always busy		
Personal relations scales		
Most people here seem to be especially considerate of others	3·83	1·85
Sociability	4·27	3·05
There is a lot of group spirit		
Social events get a lot of enthusiasm and support		
Interpersonal aggression	2·52	1·78
There always seem to be a lot of little quarrels going on here		
Homogeneity	1·54	1·09
There are many differences in nationality, religion, and social status here		

Scale title	Mean	*SD*
Routine scales		
Rules orientation	3·95	1·62
Formal rules and regulations have a very important place here		
People ask permission before deviating from common policies or practices		
Administrative efficiency	3·53	2·49
Work is well organized and progresses systematically from week to week		
The flow of information downwards is smooth and efficient		
Conventionality	5·97	2·81
There is a general idea of appropriate dress which everyone follows		
People are always carefully dressed and neatly groomed		
Readiness to innovate	3·91	2·40
New ideas are always being tried out here		
Unusual or exciting plans are encouraged here		
Variety in physical environment	2·34	1·47
Much has been done with pictures, curtains, colours and decoration to make this place pleasing to the eye		
Community scale		
Orientation to wider community	5·34	2·95
This place has a reputation for being indifferent to the needs of the wider community		
It's easy to find people here to give talks to clubs and social groups		

8 Relationships of perceptions of organizational climate to organizational structure, context, and hierarchical position*

ROY L. PAYNE and ROGER MANSFIELD

Writers on organizational behaviour recognize the need to develop a theoretical framework that allows systematic movement from one level of analysis to another (Udy, 1965; Pugh et al., 1963). The concept of organizational climate would appear to be a possible conceptual linkage between analysis at the organizational level and analysis at the individual level, and may be elaborated within frames of reference centred upon either of these two levels of analysis.

The main purpose of this paper is to examine the relationships among contextual, structural, and climate variables at the organizational level of analysis, while examining the effect of the position of individuals in the organizational hierarchy on perceptions of climate.

Variables and hypotheses

Organizational structure

Most approaches to the study of organizational structure have been based either on Weber's (1946) ideas of bureaucracy or on ideas about the management of organizations of writers such as Gulick and Urwick (1937) and Fayol (1949). Pugh and his associates (1968) at the University of Aston combined both these approaches in their attempt to design reliable measures of different aspects of organizational structure as a first step away from reliance on case studies or armchair theorizing. They

---

* edited extracts from a paper originally published in *Administrative Science Quarterly*, vol. 18, 1973, pp. 515–26.

constructed different scales to measure aspects of five primary dimensions of organizational structure; namely, specialization, formalization, standardization, centralization, and configuration (Pugh et al., 1968). From the many scales, they focused on 16 which they said best represented the variations in the total data. They used three scales as an easily applied, short-form measure of organizational structure: (1) functional specialization, the extent to which organizations specialize their nonworkflow activities along functional lines; (2) formalization of role definition, the extent to which organizations possess and distribute documents to define organizational roles; and (3) lack of autonomy, the extent to which organizational decisions are taken at levels above the chief executive, for example, by the board of a company or by a parent company.

The first and third of these measures were included in the 16 scales used in the main analysis of the Aston data; the second measure was a subscale of the overall formalization scale (Inkson et al., 1970). In the present study, a fourth measure was used as well, namely, chief-executive's span of control, the number of persons reporting directly to the senior executive officer of the organization.

Organizational context

The term organizational context is used here in the specialized and somewhat limited sense used by Pugh et al. (1969), and the measures used were: (1) organizational size, the logarithm of the number of organizational employees; (2) size of parent organization, the logarithm of the total number of employees in the parent organization of which the organization studied is a part; (3) age of the organization, in years; (4) workflow integration, a measure of technological complexity; and (5) dependence, a measure of the organization's lack of independence from other organizations. The first three were used in the original Aston study, the last two measures were detailed in the appendix to Inkson et al. (1970).

Organizational climate

The measure of organizational climate used in this study is a modified version of the Business Organization Climate Index (BOCI), developed by Payne and Pheysey (Chapter 7) from the Organization Climate Index developed by Stern (1967). In this study, the BOCI consisted of 160 statements describing various aspects of the structure and functioning of a work organization. Each respondent was asked to rate each statement as either true or false as describing the organization in which he worked. These 160 items were designed to form 20 eight-item scales. The names of

135

Table 8.1
BOCI scales, examples of items, means, standard deviations, and mean item analysis ($N = 387$)

Scale title and examples	Mean	SD	Mean item analysis
1 *Leaders' psychological distance* Senior personnel are frequently jealous of their authority.	3·60	1·87	·64
2 *Questioning authority* People who get pushed around here are expected to fight back.	4·50	1·83	·58
3 *Egalitarianism* There are no favourites in this place – everyone gets treated alike.	4·14	2·73	·80
4 *Management concern for employee involvement* Senior personnel will go out of their way to help you with your work.	4·73	2·32	·72
5 *Open-mindedness* People here speak out openly.	4·43	2·30	·69
6 *Emotional control* People here tend to hide their deeper feelings from each other.	3·32	1·69	·65
7 *Future orientation* The ability to plan ahead is highly valued here.	4·14	2·07	·68
8 *Scientific and technical orientation* A discussion about the latest scientific inventions would not be uncommon here.	3·37	2·25	·71
9 *Intellectual orientation* Careful reasoning and clear logic are highly valued here.	3·41	2·05	·70
10 *Job challenge* Most activities present a real personal challenge.	4·21	1·96	·64
11 *Task orientation* People here follow the maxim 'business before pleasure'.	3·68	2·06	·66
12 *Industriousness* There is so much to do here that people are always busy.	4·24	2·44	·75
13 *Altruism* Most people here seem to be especially considerate of others.	4·31	2·27	·70
14 *Sociability* There is a lot of group spirit.	2·85	2·09	·70
15 *Interpersonal aggression* There always seem to be a lot of little quarrels going on here.	3·94	2·34	·77
16 *Rules orientation* Formal rules and regulations have a very important place here.	3·75	1·53	·64
17 *Administrative efficiency* Work is well organized and progresses systematically from week to week.	3·47	2·30	·74
18 *Conventionality* People are always carefully dressed and neatly groomed.	4·30	1·95	·65
19 *Readiness to innovate* New ideas are always being tried out here.	3·64	2·06	·71
20 *Orientation to wider community* It's easy to find people here to give talks to clubs and social groups	3·88	2·02	·67

the scales are listed in Table 8.1 with an item illustrating each scale.

The acceptability of the scales on psychometric grounds was evaluated before using the scale scores for further analyses. The first, and perhaps most important, criterion used was face validity; that is, items that were to be added to provide a composite measure of some aspect of organizational climate had to tap highly similar content. The second criterion was that each of the items should have some amount of variance in common with the other items in the scale taken together; that is, each item should have a correlation with the scale as a whole (including that item) noticeably greater than the reciprocal of the square root of the number of items in the scale.

The first of these two criteria was applied in the construction of the BOCI. Application of the second criterion, using the data from the present study, was carried out by using item analysis and computing the Brogden-Clemens coefficient (Brogden, 1949) as the measure of association, and led to the rejection of 3 of the 160 items, shortening 3 of the climate scales to 7 items. The mean values in the item analysis for each of the 20 climate scales, after rejection of the 3 inadequate items, are shown in Table 8.1.

Relation of structure and context to climate

In the study most comparable to the present one, Payne and Pheysey (Chapter 7) used an earlier version of the BOCI and the full Aston measures of organizational structure to study differences in organizational climate among three organizations. Comparing the climate scores in two organizations approximately matched for size and technology, they found that the organization which was more centralized and bureaucratic scored higher on the climate scales measuring questioning authority, future orientation, scientific and technical orientation, intellectual orientation, job challenge, task orientation, industriousness, altruism, rules orientation, administrative efficiency, conventionality and readiness to innovate; but lower on the climate scales measuring leaders' psychological distance and orientation to wider community. Comparing the more bureaucratic of these with a third organization approximately matched on the main structural variables and employing similar technologies, but about eight times larger, the smaller organization had significantly higher scores on the climate scales measuring management concern for employee involvement, open-mindedness, future orientation, scientific and technical orientation, intellectual orientation, task orientation, industriousness, sociability, rules orientation, administrative efficiency, and readiness to innovate; but it had a lower score on the climate scale measuring leaders' psychological distance.

However, their study involved relatively unusual combinations of structural and contextual similarities and differences in the three organizations studied. Generalizations from these earlier results would be dangerous, but the studies do suggest worthwhile hypotheses.

Hypotheses

Organizational size seems a crucial variable, and it is hypothesized that, all other things being equal, larger organizations will have scores higher on the climate scales related to scientific and intellectual pursuits because of the greater number and diversity of professionals they employ. The greater economic resources are also likely to lead to their having a higher perceived concern for the involvement of their employees and a greater readiness to innovate in technological affairs. Increased bureaucratization with the large size, however, is likely to lead to climates where interpersonal aggression, emotional control, and leaders' psychological distance are higher, and to a climate more concerned with rules and following rules. Large organizations are also expected to take part in altruistic activities such as fund raising, and to be more concerned with their relations with the wider community. It is expected that the correlations between organizational size and the climate variables will be the strongest. However, as size is related to aspects of structure (Pugh et al., 1968), there will also be correlations between the structural variables of specialization and role definition and the climate variables, although these will tend to be fewer in number and weaker.

There is some evidence (Pugh et al., 1969) that organizations that are dependent (a contextual variable) are more centralized (a structural variable). Because of the restriction on authority that dependence and centralization bring, these variables are expected to be associated with greater emotional control, interpersonal aggression, and more psychologically distant leaders. Because of the increased resources often available from larger parent organizations, it is also expected that dependence may be related to readiness to innovate, and to a climate where management appears concerned for the involvement of its employees. It is not expected that these contextual and structural variables will be related to the climate scales dealing with work, that is, task orientation and industriousness. However, increased centralization of authority is expected to lead to decreased job challenge, as is formalization. Both these variables are hypothesized to reduce the autonomy of the individual and thus decrease feelings of doing challenging work.

Two studies (Pugh et al., 1969, and Child and Mansfield, 1972) have shown that the measures of technology and organization structure used in the present study are correlated at a low level. The relationships between technology (workflow integration) and climate may, therefore, be little affected by structural factors. However, there is little past research that clarifies relationships between technology and climate. Woodward (1965) found that interpersonal relationships were more harmonious in more complex technologies. Workflow integration could then be expected to be negatively related to emotional control, interpersonal aggression, and leaders' psychological distance, and positively related to questioning authority. The more complex technologies might also lead to a climate higher on the scales of scientific and technical orientation, and readiness to innovate.

Payne and Pheysey (Chapter 7) also found that more bureaucratic companies had smaller variances on the climate scales, and they suggested that increasing bureaucratization would lead to greater agreement about the work environment and produce smaller variances. However, it has already been argued in this paper that larger size, and therefore more bureaucratization, leads to a greater diversity of personnel; it is hypothesized, therefore, that size will tend to be positively correlated with variances on climate scores. If size is held constant, the hypothesis about bureaucratization may be sustained.

The original hypothesis of the Payne and Pheysey study was also that centralization and dependency would tend to narrow the range of perceptions in the company, due to the increased control implied. Results already quoted in the present paper indicate that this hypothesis may not be sustained.

The final hypothesis is that people at different levels in the organization will view the organizational climate differently. This implies that using one score to represent organizational climate may be misleading, and that relationships between the contextual and structural variables with the climate variables may differ by level. Schneider (1972) and Gorman and Malloy (1972) have found that different levels of personnel do have different views of the climate. Indeed, in a study of insurance agencies, Schneider found only very low positive correlations between the perceptions of managers, assistant managers, and agents.

Sample and method

The data reported here were collected in 14 different work organizations

139

ranging in size from 262 employees to 18,000 employees, making the following products, and having the status indicated (b = branch, hb = head branch, s = subsidiary):

golf balls (hb)	262	automotive valves (b)	750
heavy-duty electrical		screws, nuts and washers (s)	875
equipment (s)	279	gas stoves (s)	1,500
motorcycle accessories (hb)	350	retail store (b)	1,600
metal architectural fittings (s)	492	motor bodies (b)	3,200
metal plating (s)	495	motor transmissions (b)	4,580
paints (b)	500	electrical equipment (s)	18,000
aluminium castings (b)	743		

Table 8.2
Hierarchical levels as defined by the Aston paradigm

Rank above lowest level	Level	Example in manufacturing company	Number answering question- naire $N = 387$
4	Whole organization	Managing director	9
3	All workflow activities	Production manager	14
2	Workflow subunit	Plant manager	82
1	Supervisory	Foreman	87
0	Operating	Direct worker	195

In each organization the structural and contextual measures were obtained from an interview with the chief executive as described in Inkson et al. (1970), and documentary evidence collected wherever possible to verify the scores allotted. In each of the organizations an attempt was made to obtain responses to the BOCI questionnaire from line personnel at each level in the hierarchy. For comparability, hierarchical levels were defined in terms of the Aston paradigm (Pugh et al., 1968, p. 77), as shown in Table 8.2. At each level, an attempt was made to get a random, representative sample of employees to complete the climate questionnaire, except at level 4, where all chief executives were asked to respond. At level 1, at least 10 supervisors were selected to participate; at level 0, at least 25 operators were selected. Those approached did not always complete the questionnaires, as some of the companies only permitted a postal study.

Thus, the sample at the lowest levels is random, but not fully representative. In total, 387 respondents completed the questionnaire, the number from each organization ranging from 8 to 46.

Table 8.3 provides the intercorrelations among the structural and contextual variables. In general, the relationships found seem to be broadly similar to those found in other comparable studies (Pugh et al., 1968 and 1969; Inkson et al., 1970; Child, 1972a), except that the technological variable workflow integration has a stronger relationship to the structural variables of functional specialization and formalization of role definition, and organizational size has a weaker relationship with these structural variables.

Organizational scores on the climate scales were calculated by taking a grand average, and a weighted average. The weighted average was the average of the average score at each hierarchical level, and was used by Hage and Aiken (1967) to avoid having the views of lower-level personnel have too much weight because of their larger numbers. Correlations, scale by scale, between these two mean scores were high, and only 2 of the 20

Table 8.3

Intercorrelations among the structural and contextual variables*

	1	2	3	4	5	6	7	8	9
1 Functional specialization									
2 Formalization of role definition	67								
3 Lack of autonomy	—04	—40							
4 Chief executive's span of control	44	50	02						
5 Organizational size	34	53	—63	44					
6 Size of parent organization	14	38	—57	38	58				
7 Age	65	17	33	12	05	—21			
8 Workflow integration	68	36	17	39	29	10	28		
9 Dependence	30	40	23	35	11	38	—06	20	

* Decimal points omitted.

scales fell below 0·75, the median correlation being 0·87. The two lowest correlations were on the scales of emotional control (0·61) and interpersonal aggression (0·60), aspects of climate that might be more affected by individual differences than most.

Results

Analysis of variance of the organizational climate scores

It is to be expected that a one-way analysis of variance of the climate scores of individuals by organization would indicate in most cases that differences between organizations account for more of the variance than would be likely to occur from chance fluctuations. When this analysis of variance was carried out, the F ratio indicated significant (5 per cent) differences between organizations for 18 of the 20 climate scales, no significant differences being found for the scales measuring emotional control and altruism.

Organizational context, structure, and organizational climate

Table 8.4 shows the correlations between the contextual and structural dimensions and the 20 climate scales. The correlations in parentheses were based on mean scores weighted by hierarchical level. Correlations are only shown if they account for at least 10 per cent of the variance. The use of a mean score weighted by level seems to be supported by the empirical results: 67 correlations account for more than 10 per cent of the variance using the weighted mean, but only 47 using the overall mean. Moreover, there are twice as many correlations at the 5 per cent confidence level with the weighted mean (18 versus 9).

Organizational size did have a strong effect on perceived organizational climate, many of the relationships being in the direction hypothesized. Larger organizations did create climates rating higher on the work-related scales of scientific and technical orientation, intellectual orientation, job challenge, and readiness to innovate. Leaders were also seen as being more distant psychologically, although the company was seen as being concerned about the involvement of its employees. Size was also associated with the predicted concern with rules, which was supported by a high rating on conventionality, and administrative efficiency. The tendency for larger organizations to generate social clubs and the like was reflected in the correlation with sociability. Contrary to predictions, larger organizations seemed to have less interpersonal aggression, though

Table 8.4

Relationships between structural and contextual variables and organizational mean climate scores ($N = 14$; correlations are shown only if they account for more than 10 per cent of variance)**

Climate scale	Functional specialization	Formalization of role definition	Lack of autonomy	Chief executive's span of control	Log. size	Log. parent size	Age	Work-flow integration	Dependence
Leader's psychological distance			−43		34			−53*	
			(−54)*		(37)			(−35)	(−39)
Questioning authority					36		33		
	(41)				(35)		(34)	(35)	(46)
Egalitarianism								36	
			(35)	(−34)				(38)	
Management concern for employee involvement					35	42			
					(34)	(32)	(32)		
Open-mindedness						35			
						(42)			(46)
Emotional control				45					
					(34)				
Future orientation					45	39			
					(34)				
Scientific and technical orientation	43	32			53*	69*		39	57*
	(54)*	(41)			(46)	(69)*		(48)	(65)*
Intellectual orientation	34				48	43		40	45
					(35)	(58)*		(54)*	(47)
Job challenge			−36		70*	50			
	(49)		(−32)		(59)*	(57)*		(46)	
Task orientation					36				
	(47)			(40)	(41)			(34)	(36)
Industriousness									
	(32)							(35)	
Altruism									
		(34)				(53)*			(61)*
Sociability	33	42			52	51			48
		(51)			(48)	(64)*		(51)	
Interpersonal aggression					−46	−49			−42
	(−38)				(−41)	(−36)			(−48)
Rules orientation					36				
					(32)		(34)		
Administrative efficiency					30	36			
					(48)			(35)	
Conventionality			−35		43				−37
			(−36)		(36)				(−63)*
Readiness to innovate					48	66*			37*
	(35)				(65)*				(55)*
Orientation to wider community		39	−62*		78*	70*			
		(39)	(−60)*		(77)*	(70)*			

** Decimal points omitted.
* Indicates $p < ·05$.

143

this is reflected only in the overall average correlation. The weighted average showed a correlation in the predicted direction with emotional control, but as there were no correlations with open-mindedness, these relationships with the process-related scales seem unstable. The positive correlation between size and questioning authority was not predicted. Indeed, the writings of Merton (1940) and others would have suggested that larger organizations would have created enough conformity to have ruled out such behaviour; but these results indicated that people conformed over some things, but still questioned the authority of supervisors. Since larger groups are likely to include a larger number of deviants, perhaps it is they who questioned authority.

The same relationships are nearly all reflected in the correlations between climate and size of parent. The relationship between size and an altruistic climate, which was predicted, emerges only with size of parent. Larger corporations (the correlation is even stronger with dependence) presumably develop a greater range of supportive activities, and these spread to the branch units. This relationship is reinforced by the strong relationship between both size and parent size to orientation to wider community.

It was argued earlier that the bureaucratic elements of structure would tend to be related in a similar way to those of size, but would be smaller and fewer in number. That prediction holds well for specialization, and the increasing professionalization associated with specialization does lead to more stimulating climates in the area of work itself, that is, scientific and technical orientation, intellectual orientation, job challenge, task orientation, and industriousness. Greater specialization also helps to explain the higher degree of questioning of authority in larger organizations: staff personnel are, after all, paid to question and advise.

Formalization of role definition was not associated with rules orientation and conventionality, as expected. The correlation with altruism, sociability, and orientation to community presumably derive mainly from the effect of larger size.

Also, more dependent organizations did not create a climate higher on emotional control, interpersonal aggression, and leaders' psychological distance, as expected. Leaders were seen as less distant and interpersonal aggression was lower. These two relationships were supported by the correlation with questioning authority, sociability, conventionality, and open-mindedness. The climate in dependent organizations was also more challenging intellectually and there was a greater readiness to innovate. Payne and Pheysey (Chapter 7) suggested that the more positive climate in a small bureaucracy may have been partly due to the hidden subsidy of financial, technical, and ideational resources from its large, highly respected parent company.

The relationships between climate and autonomy reflect the relationships with dependence, as hypothesized. More centralized organizations had leaders who were also perceived as less psychologically distant, and the climate was also less conventional, though these two relationships were hypothesized to be in the opposite direction. The hypothesis that lack of autonomy may lead to less challenging jobs was weakly supported. Why more centralized organizations were less oriented to the wider community is not obvious.

Woodward's (1965) finding that more integrated production technologies tended to have better interpersonal relationships is partly supported. Leaders were less psychologically distant, the climate was seen as more egalitarian, and employees were prepared to question authority. More complex technologies also seemed to lead to climates concerned with scientific and technical matters, and to a more challenging work situation.

Hypotheses were not proposed about the influence of the chief executive's span of control, and the age of the organization, on organizational climate. The relationships that appear for the span of control do not have any obvious explanation. The fact that older organizations had a slightly more rules-oriented climate is not surprising; and the lower interpersonal aggression, management concern for employees, and questioning authority perhaps implies a well-developed set of social norms.

In summary, organizational climate seems to be significantly affected by organizational size and dependence. Each of these creates a climate that is relatively involved in matters surrounding work itself. This probably derives from the greater complexity with greater size, and with the increased financial and professional resources of larger organizations, which is available even to their dependent, smaller organizations. Size has some negative effects on the social processes in the organization, in that leaders are more psychologically distant, emotional control is higher, and conventionality is higher. These are to some extent countered by the readiness to question authority, to innovate, and the higher concern of management about the involvement of employees. Most of these negative social consequences are reversed with dependency. As size and dependency are almost independent of each other, perhaps some of the most attractive climates are found in large, dependent organizations.

Hierarchical position and perception of organizational climate

To examine the effects of hierarchical level on perceptions of climate, a

Table 8.5
Mean scores on climate scales for employees at each hierarchical level, and analysis of variance across levels

	Level 0 (N = 195)	1 (N = 87)	2 (N = 82)	3 (N = 14)	4 (N = 9)	F Ratio
Leaders' psychological distance	3·99	3·59	3·09	2·21	2·22	7·28***
Questioning authority	4·47	4·47	4·57	4·29	5·11	·35
Egalitarianism	3·19	4·44	5·26	6·79	7·33	18·88***
Management concern for employee involvement	4·11	4·94	5·45	6·29	7·33	11·15***
Open-mindedness	4·04	4·56	4·84	5·29	6·78	5·22***
Emotional control	3·41	3·21	3·38	3·71	1·44	3·28**
Future orientation	3·74	4·29	4·61	4·71	6·00	5·26***
Scientific and technical orientation	3·05	3·06	3·93	5·00	5·78	7·62***
Intellectual orientation	3·09	3·60	3·72	4·00	4·89	3·36***
Job challenge	3·88	4·20	4·60	5·36	6·44	6·69***
Task orientation	3·47	3·37	4·23	4·14	5·33	4·22***
Industriousness	3·82	3·87	5·16	5·57	6·56	8·52***
Altruism	3·88	4·45	4·88	5·36	5·44	4·62***
Sociability	2·78	3·01	2·72	3·29	3·22	·48
Interpersonal aggression	4·49	3·87	3·24	2·29	1·33	9·94***
Rules orientation	3·68	3·57	3·99	4·43	4·00	1·65
Administrative efficiency	3·30	3·52	3·66	3·64	4·67	1·05
Conventionality	4·03	4·34	4·77	4·71	4·67	2·40*
Readiness to innovate	3·21	3·84	4·02	4·93	5·67	7·01***
Orientation to wider community	3·63	4·17	4·00	4·57	4·44	1·86

*p < ·05
**p < ·01
***p < ·001

one-way analysis of variance of the individual climate scores categorized by hierarchical level was conducted. The F ratios and the mean scores for all respondents at each level on each of the climate scales are shown in Table 8.5. There are differences by level on 15 of the 20 scales. Level does not seem to affect the perceived level of questioning of authority, sociability, rules orientation, administrative efficiency, and orientation to community. One surprising result is that rules orientation is not seen as greater by employees at the lower levels. The only other similar study had the same finding, however (Hall, 1963).

These results seem broadly to support the idea that persons higher in the organizational hierarchy tend to perceive their organization as (1) less authoritarian, (that is, leaders' psychological distance is seen as less; and egalitarianism, open-mindedness, and management concern for employee involvement are all seen as greater); (2) providing greater work interest, (that is, characterized by greater industriousness and by greater future, scientific and technical, intellectual and task orientations, also as providing greater job challenge); (3) more friendly (greater altruism and less interpersonal aggression), and (4) more ready to innovate. These relationships would seem broadly to fit the hypothesis.

Discussion and conclusion

A major fault of the present study is the small number of organizations studied. One could point out that, even using a weighting mean, only 18 of 180 correlations are significantly different from zero, and that perhaps the best conclusion to draw is that organizational climate is independent of organizational context and structure. However, accepting the present results as our best estimates of these relationships, the pattern of relationships, using means and level, between aspects of size and dependence are strong enough to suggest that these variables do influence climate. Furthermore, data reviewed by Porter and Lawler (1965) support the influence of size on perceived attributes of the organizational environment. Stern (1970) also reported data on a large number of studies of colleges and universities that showed that size and aspects of context, such as ownership (state, private, religious, and so forth), affected the climate. However, there is great danger in using mean scores which combine the perceptions of groups whose views may be disparate, even if the mean is weighted. Where subgroups in organizations do have different perceptions, then hypotheses about their relationships with other variables must be constructed separately.

This raises the issue as to just how homogeneous are the views of subgroups. In this study, the variances of the scores for the organizations were only slightly larger than the variances for any one hierarchical level. This suggests that before the concept of organizational climate, or any other operationalization, based upon aggregated perceptions (Hall, 1963; Hage and Aiken, 1967) can be fully useful as a description of the state of a social system, it is necessary to identify the factors that are related to an individual's particular perceptions and to take them into account when exploring the relationships between climate and other dimensions of the social system. If this is done, it may be shown that the concept of organizational climate is too gross to be useful in the prediction of the behaviour of the social system it describes. That may be predicted by examining the perceived climate which directly impinges on the individual, such as that created by his role set. Some knowledge of the pattern of role set climates in an organization may be much more useful than mean scores and variances for global climate scales.

9 Correlates of variance in perceptions of organizational climate

R. MANSFIELD and R.L. PAYNE

In Payne and Mansfield (Chapter 8), we suggested that further examination of individual variation in the perceptions of organizational climate would be an important way to develop understanding of the concept and its relationships. In this paper, we examine, using the same data base as in Chapter 8, some correlates of perceptions of climate, focusing on variance measures in addition to the usual mean scores.

In order to examine the extent to which the subjects' perceptions of organizational climate varied between organizations as opposed to within organizations, a one-way analysis of variance was carried out on each of the twenty climate scales. The results of this analysis are shown in Table 9.1. The statistic quoted is the ratio of the mean square of scores between organizations to the mean square within organizations. This table suggests that, although the ratio is always more than one and that the between organization variation is statistically significant for 15 of the 20 climate scales, the relatively small ratios indicate there must be consequential within organization variation as well. The between organization differences shown in this table indicate that climate is a legitimate concept at the organizational level (at least for 15 of the dimensions) but that internal variations in perceptions are likely to be important.

In order to examine the possible relationships between the variation in perceptions of climate found within organizations and the structure and context of the organizations the variance on each climate scale in each organizational sample was correlated with the structural and contextual measures. Those correlations, which account for more than 10 per cent of the variance, are reported in Table 9.2. As predicted there seems to be greater variation in perceptions of climate in larger organizations than in

Table 9.1
Analysis of variance of each of the climate scales by organization
($N = 387$ respondents in 14 organizations)

Climate scale	F ratio
Leaders' psychological distance	2·802***
Questioning authority	2·081**
Egalitarianism	2·749**
Management concern for employee involvement	3·439***
Open-mindedness	3·241***
Emotional control	1·046
Future orientation	4·060***
Scientific and technical orientation	6·990***
Intellectual orientation	3·903***
Job challenge	4·273***
Task orientation	1·928*
Industriousness	4·316***
Altruism	1·262
Sociability	5·476***
Interpersonal aggression	1·717
Rules orientation	2·858***
Administrative efficiency	4·206***
Conventionality	5·577***
Readiness to innovate	4·090***
Orientation to wider community	9·734***

* $p < 0.05$
** $p < 0.01$
*** $p < 0.001$

smaller ones, size accounting for more than 10 per cent of the variance on 8 of the 20 climate scales. Surprisingly the measure most obviously tapping aspects of bureaucracy, that is, formalization of role definition, also tends to be positively related to the amount of variation in organizational climate, though this is most probably due to the effect of size on formalization. The partial correlation between role definition and variability of perceptions of sociability with organizational size held constant is 0·43 compared to the zero-order correlation of 0·61. No particularly obvious pattern of relationships between variances in climate perceptions and functional specialization emerge, and only a single scale is

Table 9.2

Relationships between structural and contextual variables and variances of organizational climate scores ($N = 14$). (Correlations are only shown if they account for more than 10 per cent of variance.)
(Decimal points omitted)

Climate scale	Functional specialization	Formalization of role definition	Lack of autonomy	Chief executive's span	Log. size	Log. parent size	Age	Workflow integration	Dependence
Leader's psychological distance	–	–	–	34	–	–	–	–	–
Questioning authority	–	–	–	–	41	–	–	—45	–
Egalitarianism	—45	–	–	–	–	–	—49	–	–
Management concern for employee involvement	–	–	–	–	–	–	34	–	–
Open-mindedness	–	–	–	41	–	–	–	–	–
Emotional control	–	–	–	–	–	34	–	–	–
Future orientation	–	–	–	–	–	–	–	–	–
Scientific and technical orientation	–	–	–	–	–	34	—42	–	39
Intellectual orientation	–	36	–	–	40	50	–	–	47
Job challenge	–	–	—69*	–	69*	–	–	–	–
Task orientation	41	47	–	50	47	–	38	–	–
Industriousness	–	–	–	–	39	–	–	–	–
Altruism	–	–	–	–	–	–	–	53*	—33
Sociability	39	61*	–	47	66*	65*	–	–	69*
Interpersonal aggression	–	–	–	–	–	–	–	–	–
Rules orientation	–	–	–	–	–	–	—61*	–	–
Administrative efficiency	—64*	–	–	–	–	–	—37	–	–
Conventionality	–	–	–	–	39	–	–	–	–
Readiness to innovate	–	–	–	–	–	44	–	–	67*
Orientation to wider community	–	35	–	51	56*	–	–	–	55*

* indicates $p < 0.05$

importantly related to lack of autonomy – there is less variance in perceptions of job challenge in organizations which lack autonomy. Size of parent organization and dependence on other organizations are also related to variance in climate perceptions on a number of dimensions. In general variation is greater in more dependent organizations and in those with larger owning groups.

These results have shown that certain systematic relationships appear to obtain between the variance in perceptions of certain dimensions of climate in an organization and certain structural and contextual features of the organization. It is not clear, however, on the evidence presented so far whether these variances largely represent hierarchical differences in perceptions or general disagreements amongst persons throughout the organization. This question is potentially important as statistically significant relationships were found between hierarchical position and perceptions of climate on 15 of the 20 scales (Chapter 8). In order to examine this problem a measure of the total hierarchical difference in perceptions of climate was computed by taking the square of the difference between the average score on each scale for the managers in an organization and the average score of the operatives in that organization.

Table 9.3

Relationships between intra-organizational variance and hierarchical variations ($N = 14$)

Climate scale	Correlation
Leaders' psychological distance	57
Questioning authority	—22
Egalitarianism	19
Management concern for employee involvement	63*
Open-mindedness	45
Emotional control	—09
Future orientation	51
Scientific and technical orientation	69*
Intellectual orientation	23
Job challenge	—21
Task orientation	48
Industriousness	35
Altruism	—10
Sociability	—29
Interpersonal aggression	52
Rules orientation	01
Administrative efficiency	04
Conventionality	29
Readiness to innovate	82*
Orientation to wider community	—42

* $p < 0.05$

Although the absolute difference between the views of managers and operators indicates something useful itself, the face validity of this index is improved if the middle levels of management tend to fall between the operatives and the managers. This happens for 15 of the 20 scales, and in three of the five others the differences are very small (see Table 8.5). This measure, which we have called hierarchical variation, was in general positively correlated with the overall variance scores (Table 9.3), but not perhaps as strongly as might have been anticipated.

In fact, for 6 of the 20 scales the relationships are negative (although nonsignificant). This table makes clear that, with the possible exception of the scales measuring management concern with employee involvement, scientific and technical orientation and readiness to innovate, the relationship between hierarchical variation and total organizational variance is such that we cannot, in the main, attribute the relationships between climate variances and structure and context to hierarchical variation. In order to examine the effects of this latter variable we computed the correlations between the scores on hierarchical variation and the measures of structure and context (Table 9.4).

Comparison of Tables 9.2 and 9.4 makes clear that the patterns of relationships between structural and contextual parameters and the two measures of variation in perceptions of climate are in many respects different. Not surprisingly, lack of autonomy, which is a short form measure of centralization (Inkson et al., 1970), is more related to hierarchical variations in climate perceptions than it is to total organizational variances. In most cases lack of autonomy is positively related to hierarchical variations in perceptions, suggesting that climate perceptions may in some respects be related to decision making power. Examination of the main measure of bureaucracy, formalization of role definition, shows that it, too, is more likely to be related to hierarchical variations than to total variances in perceptions of organizational climate. Greater bureaucracy appears in general to be associated with less hierarchical variation in perceptions of climate. This result differs markedly from the paradoxical finding of the tendency for this measure of bureaucracy to be positively associated with total organizational variances in perceptions of some aspects of climate. The relationships with the other two structural variables, functional specialization and chief executives' span of control also show some differences in their relationships with the two different measures of variation in perceptions, but these differences seem less patterned and more dependent on the aspect of climate being examined.

When attention is turned to the relationships involving contextual factors,

153

Table 9.4
Relationships between structural and contextual variables and
hierarchical variation in organizational climate scores ($N = 14$).
(Correlations are only shown if they account for more than 10 per cent of
variances.) (Decimal points omitted)

Climate scale	Functional specialization	Formalizaton of role definition	Lack of autonomy	Chief executive's span	Log. size	Log. parent size	Age	Workflow integration	Dependence
Leaders' psychological distance	–	—34	–	–	—36	–	–	—34	–
Questioning authority	—62*	—52	–	—45	–	–	–	—38	—38
Egalitarianism	–	–	–	–	–	60*	–	–	53*
Management concern for employee involvement	–	—39	48	–	—38	–	–	–	–
Open-mindedness	–	—37	41	–	—50	–	–	–	–
Emotional control	–	–	–	–	–	–	–	–	–
Future orientation	–	–	–	–	–	–	–	–	–
Scientific and technical orientation	–	—32	38	–	—34	–	–	–	–
Intellectual orientation	–	–	—34	–	–	–	–	–	–
Job challenge	–	—39	–	–	–	–	—38	40	–
Task orientation	41	–	–	42	53*	–	—35	40	–
Industriousness	36	–	38	53*	–	–	–	–	–
Altruism	–	39	–	68*	–	–	—37	–	–
Sociability	–	—57*	–	—40*	–	–	–	–	—36
Interpersonal aggression	–	–	51	–	–	–	–	–	38
Rules orientation	–	–	–	–	–	–	–	–	40
Administrative efficiency	–	–	–	–	–	54*	–	–	–
Conventionality	49	–	–	49	48	–	–	51	–
Readiness to innovate	–	–	39	–	–	–	–	–	67*
Orientation to wider community	–	–	–	—38	–	–	–	–	—71*

* indicates $p < 0.05$

the most striking shift of pattern is in relationships with organizational size. The impact of size seems to be slightly less upon hierarchical variations in climate perceptions than upon total organizational variances. The effect of size seems in many cases to reduce the hierarchical variations in perceptions of climate, whereas it increased the total organizational variance in climate perceptions. These results suggest the possibility that the efforts of bureaucratic managers to bring some uniformity to the large organizations they manage has to some extent been successful. There are smaller variations in perceptions of climate between levels in large, specialized and formalized organizations. That is, the uniformity is aimed at large groups and it works, even though the greater variety of personnel that sheer size involved initially leads to greater variances in perceptions, as is revealed in Table 9.2. Size of parent organization seems to have less impact upon hierarchical variation in climate perceptions than on total organizational variance.

It was shown in Chapter 8 that significant variations were to be found in perceptions of climate by level; here it has been shown that the extent of the hierarchical variation relates to other parameters of the organizational system. In the next section we examine the relationships between structural and contextual variables and mean perceptions of climate at each organizational level. The relationships with overall organizational climate means were reported in Chapter 8. However it would seem likely that these overall relationships may hide variation in the relationships at each level. Examination of the relationships between the means for each of the levels also suggests considerable possibilities for variation in relations with other variables by level. The correlations between means for each level are all positive except for those relating to emotional control, but only in 7 cases out of 60 are the relations strong enough to predict more than 50 per cent of the variance from one level to another.

It is expected that these data will reveal the following trends:

(a) there will be stronger correlations between bureaucratic variables (size, specialization, role definition) and climate variables relating to the recruitment of personnel at the lower organizational levels.

(b) More specialized, dependent and centralized organizations are expected to create more positive climates for higher management levels, particularly in regard to job-related variables such as scientific and technical orientation, job challenge, etc.

The correlation between structural and contextual variables and climate means by level are shown in Table 9.5. The total set of relationships in this table is obviously very complicated and in general the predicted patterns do not appear to be found.

Hypothesis (a) is not substantiated at all. There is no tendency for the relationships between the climate and the structural (bureaucratic) variables to be stronger and negative at lower levels. Indeed, in the only cases where there are strongish negative relationships, the relationships are in the opposite direction to that predicted. Lower-level people in more bureaucratic organizations see the climate as less conventional and lower on emotional control. There are few differences across organizational levels associated with organizational size. One exception is the difference in

155

Table 9.5

Correlations among organizational context, structure and organizational climate dimensions by hierarchical level. $N = 14$. (Correlations quoted when one of the three values account for at least 10 per cent of variance.)
(Decimal points omitted)

	Functional specialization			Formalization of role definition			Lack of autonomy			Chief executive's span			Log. size			Log. parent size			Age			Workflow integration			Dependence		
	O*	S	M	O	S	M	O	S	M	O	S	M	O	S	M	O	S	M	O	S	M	O	S	M	O	S	M
Leaders' psychological distance							-32	-33	-55*	-03	37	41	10	11	69*							-72*	-48	-03	-37	-14	-21
Questioning authority	33	64*	28	27	54	10							39	37	24	-01	22	36	29	41	35	47	58	-15			
Egalitarianism							37	-05	39	-33	-53	-29	-25	14	-36										06	-06	34
Management concern for employee involvement				-10	03	-33	-02	-12	47	-39	-43	-07				32	54*	10							20	03	43
Open-mindedness	00	-68*	15	-49	-43	22	-25	00	33	-28	-22	-42	39	19	-28	32	58*	16				49	-40	09	10	44	30
Emotional control				-43	01	-05							-20	-22	38	-35	-49	14	06	-49	35				-41	-45	11
Future orientation										-45	-13	09	21	36	16	24	44	21									
Scientific and technical orientation	06	43	53	02	47	18							26	46	28	68*	64*	55*				-01	23	52	37	71*	55*
Intellectual orientation	00	39	45	-26	35	22	35	08	10	-32	12	42	02	24	50	11	39	55*				05	40	49	09	56*	51
Job challenge	-02	62*	23	-02	52	-05							51	42	47	27	40	58*									
Task orientation													-23	14	44	-26	18	33				-37	22	22	-23	55*	27
Industriousness																						03	18	32	05	48	25
Altruism							36	-08	22	-57*	-18	01													13	17	44
Sociability	-04	42	31	10	51	40				-38	14	14	41	29	39	46	39	52							15	60*	55*
Interpersonal aggression	-37	15	15				-07	01	-43	55*	36	22				-30	-43	-23							-24	-18	-43
Rules orientation	-18	36	11	-42	-14	-05				-46	-26	25	16	25	33	09	50	-04									
Administrative efficiency	-72	10	10	-55*	-07	02				-45	01	-28				10	42	37	01	06	43	10	39	17	-11	48	-01
Conventionality	-01	44	19	-22	46	-06	-23	08	-42	-51	-18	19	10	-09	61*							-46	34	22	-51	-35	-45
Readiness to innovate	-05	14	32	18	28	43				-45	21	-19	21	42	09	42	59*	55*							02	57*	47
Orientation to wider community							-55	-56*	-64*				65*	71*	72*	58*	75*	64*									

O indicates operative level; S indicates supervisory level; M indicates management level. * indicates $p < 0.05$

156

relationships between operators and managers on task orientation, where there is a small negative relationship (-0.23) for operators and a strong positive one for managers (0.50). As this pattern is not replicated on any of the other work-related climate scales it cannot be attributed serious credence. Managers in larger organizations see their bosses as psychologically more distant, but this is not true for supervisors or operators. If it were merely a question of remoteness the same relationship might be expected to exist in centralized and dependent organizations, but the relationship is negative in both cases, which indicates that large size in itself creates psychological distance amongst very senior managers. This is relative, of course, since in an absolute sense the level of leaders' psychological distance is lower at upper levels of the organization (cf. Chapter 8).

Hypothesis (b) comes closer to being substantiated. Future orientation, intellectual orientation, job challenge, and industriousness are all noticeably more likely to be negatively or less positively related to structural and contextual variables for operatives than for managers. This tendency is particularly true for relations with technology and to a lesser extent with organizational size. These results fit with the ideas of larger, technologically more complex organizations using more resources on planning and creating a challenging work environment particularly for higher hierarchical levels. Conventionality is also more likely to be associated negatively or less positively with structural and contextual variables for operatives than for managers. This is particularly true for relationships with specialization, formalization, chief executive's span, size and technology.

Discussion

The results reported here have shown that the intra-organizational variations in perceptions of organizational climate can themselves be meaningfully treated as parameters of the organizational system and relate to other organizational variables. Understanding of the factors which affect dispersion of climate perceptions in organizations not only provides important knowledge of the workings of organizations; it also allows us to use aggregate or average measures of climate with greater confidence and insight. The results reported here also showed that hierarchical variation in perceptions of climate was not usually strongly related to total organizational variance in perceptions. This again emphasizes the very considerable importance of hierarchy in affecting the way people see their employing organizations.

This importance of hierarchy was further emphasized when the relationships between mean perceptions of climate and structural and contextual variables were examined level by level. This examination revealed some interesting changes in relationships but definitely did not reveal a positive interaction effect between size, bureaucracy, and complex technology and low hierarchical position producing a highly negative work environment. Indeed, any tendency that was found suggested that increasing organizational size and technological complexity may actually ameliorate the organizational climate for lower-level employees.

In general, then, this paper has demonstrated that intra-organizational variations in perceptions of organizational climate are meaningfully related to other variables and that variations in relations between perceptions of climate and aspects of structure and context by level can also add to our knowledge of the way organizations function.

The approach adopted here is based on a rejection of the ideas that descriptive measures of organizations such as climate which must be assessed through the perceptions of individuals are only useful when near-unanimity is achieved amongst organizational members. Guion (1973, p. 124) has put this argument most strongly when he argues that only dichotomous items should be used and 'the items to be treated as genuinely descriptive are those in which the frequency of endorsement either is not significantly different from 100 per cent or not significantly different from 0 per cent'. We would suggest that such an approach when applied to large samples of employees scattered through large organizations is unrealistic. In fact in the present study only one of the 160 climate items was endorsed similarly by 90 per cent or more of the employees in each of the 14 organizations. Indeed, using Pace's (1963) criterion of 66 per cent agreement, only 4 of the 160 items show this level of agreement in all 14 of the organizations studied here. This does not seem surprising when one considers the vast range of experience faced by different persons with different personal characteristics in different roles in a single large organization. On the contrary it would be surprising if this range of experience did not create variation in perception even with purely descriptive items. This variation is likely to be increased in a society where everybody is exposed via the media to ideas about the 'right' and 'wrong' ways to manage and administer organizations. Under such circumstances even the purest descriptive items must take on evaluative elements.

Rather than accept the strait-jacket suggested by Guion, we would argue that it is better to use both the mean (weighted or not) and measures of dispersion when using empirical evidence relating to concepts like organizational climate. And that where meaningful differences occur in organizations, such as between levels or departments, the same statistical indices may be used to comprehend more fully the behaviour of organizations and their influence on the people working in them.

10 Concluding remarks

In this chapter we summarize the results of the studies reported and present an alternative conceptual framework, based on 'facet analysis', for classifying the measures used and clarifying the relationships between them. After examining the evidence on the reliability and validity of the measures, we offer an overall evaluation of the attempt to relate group and individual level variables to organizational context and structure.

The results of the studies in this volume

Following Hickson's demonstration (Chapter 1) of the importance of 'specificity of role prescription' in the thinking of organizational theorists, Inkson et al. (Chapter 2) developed measures of role definition and routine and perceived interpersonal conflict and innovative role sending. They related these measures to structural dimensions using the 'administrative reduction of variance' thesis. This hypothesizes that high structuring of activities and centralization of authority is related to greater role definition and routine and less conflict and innovation, as perceived by the managers. The data show that the relationships with centralization support the hypothesis but with small correlations, whereas the relationships with structuring of activities go clearly in the opposite direction to those hypothesized.

The papers by Child (Chapter 3) and Child and Ellis (Chapter 4) report a replication of this study on a much larger sample of managers in twice as many organizations. Psychometric examination of the measures replicated the original characteristics quite well. The results showed again that the relationships between centralization and routine and conforming behaviour supported the model, whereas those with structuring of activities did not, as far as role routine is concerned. But they did in relation to role formalization and role definition. These differences led Child to suggest that Hickson's concept of role specificity is multi-dimensional, with different aspects of role related to different aspects of structure.

One general conclusion from the studies in Part I is clear. The negative psychological consequences of bureaucracy predicted by many writers on organizations do not appear in any strong and consistent way in these data on senior managers. This prompts the hypothesis that these effects have their full force at lower levels in the organization. It may be that these senior managers are above the full force of the bureaucratic system.

The group studies in Part II allow a test of this hypothesis. They report an aspect of the Aston programme which has often been neglected owing to the concentration on organizational level studies reported in the first two volumes of this series. The aim of this aspect of the programme was to carry out in-depth studies of groups and individuals in organizations with known structures and contexts. They illustrate the value of this approach by allowing some explanation of the complex relationships found at the group level of analysis. Thus 'Aston', the small, effective bureaucracy, created a considerable degree of similarity in group structure and functioning which permeated all levels of the organizational hierarchy. In the less structured organization, 'Brum', there was a greater variety of group functioning and no obvious relationship with level in the hierarchy. The effect of decentralization but with a long hierarchy in 'Brum' provides an interesting example of the counteracting effects of different structural variables. As the further comparisons with 'Carrs' show, generalizations about the unitary effects of bureaucratic structure on behaviour are inadequate since such effects may work in different directions.

Thus the administrative reduction of variance thesis does not apply in any simple way at the lower levels of management and supervision, although its effects may be traced along with other factors. The group studies, along with the role studies, show that bureaucratic structures can provide, satisfying work environments. As the contingency approach would suggest, it is a matter of getting the balance of factors right, and 'Aston' is one organization which appears to have achieved that.

The climate studies in Part III have developed a reasonably good climate measure, but the empirical studies as yet lack sufficient numbers of organizations to allow confidence that all the relationships found will be replicated. Nevertheless it is clear that organizational parameters do have an effect on certain dimensions of climate: for example, greater size is associated with intellectual orientation, functional specialization with scientific and technical orientation, autonomy with leaders' psychological distance. One's position in the hierarchy clearly affects one's perception of the climate.

The climate studies have also demonstrated (Chapter 9) that there is value in using indices of variance as well as means in exploring the relationships between context, structure and climate. This is a useful contribution to the conceptual discussion about the measurement of organizational climate and the problems of aggregating subjective data. In general the climate studies, too, show no evidence that less attractive climates consistently occur in bureaucratic structures, which gives some consistency to the complexity obtained through the three forms of studies – role, group and climate – which have been presented.

Organizational structure, roles and climate as constructs

The summary of the results given above takes for granted that the measures used in the studies are reliable and valid. One aspect of validity ('construct validity') is that the measures represent well the characteristics under study. It is thus an important first step in evaluation to clarify the conceptual basis of the characteristics being considered and to examine the adequacy of the constructs being used to represent them.

In Payne and Pugh (1976) we distinguished between organizational structure and organizational climate each defined as in the present volume. In addition, however, we argued that each of these two concepts can be operationally measured through both subjective and objective means, and further that it is important to be clear about the relationship between a concept and its operational measure, since relationships between different types of measures of the same constructs will not be exactly the same. These distinctions were first made in Chapter 7, but their application to climate and structure leads us to reconceptualize some of the measures used in organizational research including some of the role variables referred to in Part I.

As we pointed out (Payne and Pugh, 1976), some of the dimensions of organizational climate measures might be more usefully conceived as subjective measures of dimensions of organizational structure. This is not just academic neatness, but is vital to testing out hypotheses about how to change organizations, since it is important to be clear whether measures represent independent variables such as structures (which are often manipulated) or intervening variables such as climate (which often change as a result of the manipulation) or dependent variables such as performance (changes in which can also affect the intervening variables). Climate itself might be the dependent variable, but the important point is to have concepts clear and operationalizations of them just as clear.

Payne et al. (1976) used facet analysis (Guttman, 1954) to elucidate the nature of measures surrounding the concepts of climate and job satisfaction. They were able to show that eight concepts were needed to describe the various measures so far developed, and also that authors had

Unit of analysis						JOB						ROLE						ORGANIZATION					
Concept				Structure			Climate			Structure			Climate			Structure			Climate		
Measurement				Subject-ive		Object-ive	Subject-ive		Object-ive	Subject-ive		Object-ive	Subject-ive		Object-ive	Subject-ive		Object-ive	Subject-ive		Object-ive
Data source																					
Data type	1	Individual's perception of job characteristics	Single																			
	2	Group's perception of X's job characteristics	Many																			
	3	Job description/analysis																				
	4	Individual's perception of job climate	Single																			
	5	Group's perception of X's job climate	Many																			
	6	Objective job climate (independent observer, film, etc.)																				
	7	Individual's perception of a role's structure	Single																			
	8	Group's perception of a role's structure	Many																			
	9	Objective role description																				
	10	Individual's perception of a role's climate	Single																			
	11	Group's perception of a role's climate	Many																			
	12	Objective description of a role's climate																				
	13	Individual's perception of organization structure (Hemphill)	Single																			
	14	Group's perception of organizational structure (Hemphill)	Many																			
	15	Objective organization structure (Aston)																				
	16	Individual's perception of organizational climate	Single																			
	17	Group's perception of organizational climate	Many																			
	18	Objective organizational climate																				

Fig. 10.1   Facet analysis of the measures used in the study of structure, roles and climate

163

not always distinguished the actual concept to which their measure related. This led, it was argued, to inferior measures as well as confusion in the testing of theoretical propositions.

Since facet analysis proved helpful in that instance, it may also help to distinguish the measures used in the study of structure, roles and climate. Figure 10.1 presents a facet analysis of what appear to be the relevant facets connected with this problem: the unit of analysis (job, role or social organization), the concept (structure or climate), the nature of the measurement (subjective or objective), and, for the subjective measurement only, the data source, which means whether the data were from a single individual or from more than one individual (usually that would mean several or many).

This last distinction does not apply to 'objective data', since it is assumed that these are instances where many would agree that something was true, was publicly observable, etc. In practice both 'subjective' and 'objective' data from more than one person are subject to limitations and distortions, and Barker (1965), who has developed most fully the operationalization of subjective and objective data, actually suggests a continuous variation between them, rather than a dichotomy. Social science is not objective to the same degree as physical science, but the distinction seems worthy of making even if it is not as clear cut as we would like it to be.

The facet analysis in Figure 10.1 generates eighteen concepts, many of which have been operationalized in the studies in this volume. Spelling them out does clarify what has been done and helps to make the findings easier to evaluate.

In the facet analysis we have distinguished between job and role. Job refers to the job an *individual* does. There may be other individuals who do the same activities under the same organizational rules etc., but when looking at any individual we have said he has a job. We have used the term role to refer to what more than one person does (i.e. the inspector's role, the clerk's role, or the manager's role). If we apply this to the role measures in Part I, we can see that the top managers in each company have a specialist job different from the specialist jobs of their colleagues. Thus, when Child (Chapter 3) analyzes the data from his 787 respondents and they are describing the role formalization, role definition etc., in their *jobs*, the measure is a Type 1 measure according to the facet analysis. When the data are aggregated to represent each organization, they actually represent a more general role in organizations – that of manager. That is, conceptually it would be inappropriate to aggregate different jobs (specialist jobs), but if one allows the role of manager to be common to all the specialist jobs, then one can aggregate these Type 1 data and this converts them into Type 8 — Group perceptions of a role's structure.

The behavioural variables of questioning authority, pressing for change, and conflict are perceptions of the behaviour of other managers in their managerial roles. When used as measures at the individual level, these scores are Type 10 (Individual's perceptions of the role climate) and when aggregated to represent the organization they are actually representing top management role climate (Type 11). To emphasize the complexity of these data it is worth noting that the expected behaviour variables in the Inkson and Child studies ask about the extent to which *the respondent thinks* his colleagues should do something, and do not fall within the framework of the facet analysis. Strictly speaking these are individual difference variables, though when they are aggregated one might be justified in claiming that they represent some aspect of the role's climate (Type 11) in that they reflect prevalent values. Child did not call his measures climate measures at all, but left them defined as behavioural variables. Since no actual behaviour is measured here, but reports of abstractions of behaviour, we feel that such measures are better described as climate measures, and they certainly fall within the definition of climate offered in the Introduction.

To complete our analysis of the types of data in this volume, we have to recognise that the Aston structural measures are Type 15, that the Business Organization Climate Index (Chapter 7) is Type 17, that the data on managerial groups (Chapter 5) include Type 14 (Group's perceptions of the structure of the social organization of the group), and Type 17 (Group's perceptions of its climate).

The value of facet analysis is that it clarifies and organizes this conceptual complexity. It achieves organization by the use of two principles (Foa, 1965): the principle of contiguity which proposes that facets which are more similar conceptually will be more closely related; and the principle of hierarchy, which suggests that the facets can be arranged in a hierarchical order of importance. On the basis of these two principles one can suggest a conceptual structure for the data which can then be tested empirically by seeing whether those facets which are conceptually contiguous are more highly related to each other. Figure 10.1 has been constructed on the basis that the facets at the top of the diagram are more important than those at the bottom – they are in descending order of hierarchical relevance. That is, the unit of analysis (job, role or organization) is regarded as more fundamental than the concept (structure or climate), which is in turn more basic than the nature of the

165

measurement (subjective–objective), and the source of data (single person or many persons) remains important, but less important than the other facets.

Following Payne et al. (1976), a simple numerical weighting can be used to estimate the conceptual contiguity of every type of concept with every other. Table 10.1 shows the weightings given to the facets in the Child study. Each facet is compared to every other and by giving the relationship a weighting of 4 when the unit of analysis is common to both facets, 3 when the concept is common, 2 when the measurement method is common and 1 when the data source is common, a crude estimate of the conceptual contiguity is calculated. Thus Table 10.2 proposes that Types 7 and 8 are conceptually more similar than any other pair and that this should be reflected in a stronger empirical relationship. Types 10 and 15, and 11 and 15 will be the weakest relationships if the hypothesis built into the facet analysis is correct.

Table 10.1
Data types and their conceptual contiguity

Data types		Numerical weighting
1 and 7	=	6
1 and 8	=	5
1 and 10	=	3
1 and 11	=	2
1 and 15	=	2
7 and 8	=	9
7 and 10	=	7
7 and 11	=	6
7 and 15	=	3
8 and 10	=	6
8 and 11	=	7
8 and 15	=	3
10 and 11	=	9
10 and 15	=	0
11 and 15	=	0

We do not have the data to test out all these relationships but enough are available to assess its potential. Table 10.1 suggests that the objective measures of structure (Type 15) are more contiguous to the structure of roles subjectively perceived by the managers (Type 8) than they are to the perceived role climate (Type 11). Their weightings are 3 and zero respectively. Tables 3.5 and 3.6 of Child show that empirically there are more and larger relationships between Type 15 and Type 8 measures than between Type 15 and Type 11 measures. Twenty-one out of 36 correlations reach the 95 per cent confidence level or beyond in the former case, whereas only 6 out of 30 do so in the latter.

Applying the same comparison to the Inkson et al. study (Chapter 2) one has to take account of the fact that there are fewer measures of each type: the structural measures are summarized as factors and only two role and climate variables are presented. Thus in Table 2.2 there are only 8 correlations available to test the hypothesis. The result is less clear cut though in the predicted direction: the average correlation for the Types 15 and 8 comparison is 0·31, whereas the average for the Types 15 and 11 comparison is 0·27.

Child (Chapter 3) refers to the possible distortions in his analysis at the organizational level as a result of using the mean of the individual's descriptions of their jobs to represent the managerial role's structure and climate. The facet analysis suggests a contiguity score of 5 between Type 1 (the individual's perception of his job characteristics) and Type 8 (the group's perceptions of the managerial role's structure). If this relationship of moderate size does exist empirically, then it implies that the relationships at the organizational level will be inflated in size due to the contamination of this individual level relationship. Table 4.8 of Ellis and Child includes correlations for the 787 individuals and for the 78 organizations. These bear out the prediction of the facet analysis since the correlations at the organizational level are larger than at the individual level, but the latter are large enough to be having an effect on the organizational level relationships. The real size of the organizational level relationships can only be estimated by partialling out for the individual effects as was done in Pheysey et al. in Table 5.4.

Table 10.1 indicates two other large relationships: individual's perception of the role structure and the group's perception of the role structure (Types 7 and 8), and individual's perceptions of a role's climate and group's perceptions of a role's climate (Types 10 and 11). Unfortunately the analyses of these relationships are not available, but the implicit hypothesis is that close contact with colleagues will in general influence one's perceptions of role and climate. Payne and Mansfield

167

(1975) have shown that the average views of colleagues do have an influence on an individual's perception of the total organization climate. It seems not unlikely that the effects will be even stronger in small managerial groups.

This brings us back to the purposes of the facet analysis. The first purpose is in helping us to see exactly what concepts our measures represent. It has revealed to us, for example, that in Payne and Pugh (1976) it was inaccurate to classify the role variables as subjective measures of organizational structures, and the behaviour and expectation variables as subjective measures of organizational climate. However, as the contiguity scores for the two relationships are both 6 (i.e. Types 8 and 14, and Types 11 and 17), it is unlikely that our interpretations were too misleading.

The second purpose of the facet analysis is to provide hypotheses about the structure of the data which can be tested empirically. Support for our hypothesis lends credence both to the measures and to the underlying structure of the theory. It is encouraging that, by and large, the results conform to the structure suggested by the facet analysis, although further testing out is required. The analysis also reveals that the relationships found at the organizational level between organizational structure, role structure and role climate are larger than the 'true' collectivity relationships, being inflated by the relationship between role structure and role climate, at the individual level. Correction for this in the analysis may change some of the significance of the relationships used in the path analysis (Child, Chapter 3) which may lead to changes in the interpretation of the proposed processes of control.

Facet analysis is, of course, not concerned with the empirical content of the findings. It is a useful tool for conceptually clarifying the data with which we deal. It can point out discrepancies in the structure and relationships of the data and suggest improvements. When, as in the present case, the data structure in general bears out the analysis, it provides some confidence that the substantive meaning of the relationships found can be explored in the knowledge that the data structure is stable.

Discussion of the meaning of empirical relationships is predicated not only on the conceptual clarity of the constructs, but also on the acceptable reliability and validity of the measures. The context and structure variables were considered in the previous volumes (Pugh and Hickson, 1976; Pugh and Hinings, 1976). We now discuss these aspects of the role, group and climate measures.

Reliability and validity of role measures

No data exist about the internal reliability of the role variables, nor the test–retest reliability, but experience with questionnaires of this type would suggest that those dimensions derived from large principal components are likely to have acceptable reliability. Some of the other scales, however, are composed of only two or three items which have low levels of intercorrelation between them and these scales might prove less reliable. The questioning authority scales for both perceived and expected behaviour are the most obvious examples.

Even though they have high face validity, these shorter scales also come into question in terms of their construct validity. As Child and Ellis show (Chapter 4), there are significant differences amongst various industries on all these dimensions. This suggests that these smaller factors may change if the items were used on samples of top managers in different industries, or if they were used on managers and supervisors from lower levels of the organizations.

Payne and Pugh (1976) compared the objective measures of organizational structure with the subjective measures of role structure for the Inkson et al. study (Chapter 2), the Child and Ellis study (Chapter 4) and another study by Inkson et al. (1971) which used the same variables in a study of managers in 17 US organizations. They commented that the two ways of operationalizing structuring of activities (i.e. objective and subjective) showed only moderate relationships with each other, but the two ways of operationalizing centralization of authority were more strongly correlated. There is certainly need for the development of more accurate measures of the two aspects of structure which will show greater convergent validity with each other, but the developments seem to be in the right direction.

Reliability and validity of measures of groups in organizations

Apart from the Hemphill Group Dimensions Description Questionnaire (1956) used in the Pheysey et al. study (Chapter 5), there is little to add about the reliability and validity of the group measures. Pheysey and Payne (1970) in a detailed examination of the reliability and validity of the Hemphill measures as used in the present studies, noted that one scale, permeability, proved unsuitable for the particular sample used, and four were rejected as insufficiently unidimensional. The remaining eight scales were found to be meaningful both in terms of concurrent and predictive validity. But some of the measures consist of only single items, so that much work could be done to improve them. This is particularly true of measures of performance which have the intrinsic problem of being applicable only to groups doing the same task. Fiedler's (1971) work on leadership of groups has shown that the group's performance is contingent on having appropriate styles of leadership to match the characteristics of the groups led (the social relationships, the tasks done and the power of the leader's authority). His measures are not well researched as to their psychometric properties, however, and further work in this direction may help to progress our understanding of work groups.

Reliability and validity of climate measures

There are now a number of measures of organizational climate many of which we referred to in Payne and Pugh (1976). Measures have been developed for specific forms of organizations – medical schools, high schools, universities, classrooms, research organizations, and business organizations. Such specialization is probably the way to go, although there are aspects of the climate of organizations which are likely to be common to all organizations and comparative research would benefit from such common concepts being included in future studies. Dimensions such as warmth and support, openness of communication, psychological distance of senior people, spring to mind as examples. Compared to these measures, the BOCI (Chapter 7) used in the Aston studies seems to measure some of these general dimensions as well as stressing some dimensions which may be of particular relevance to business organizations, such as technical orientation, administrative efficiency and orientation to wider community. In addition, BOCI contains very few scales which seem to be about structuring of activities at work and about the allocation of authority within the organization. As we have said, these are better conceptualized as subjective measures of structure. In this sense the BOCI has high face validity as a measure of dimensions of climate.

Psychometrically, the twenty scales in the BOCI have acceptable to quite good internal reliability. Test–retest reliability over short periods seems reasonable also. Another advantage of the instrument is that the mean scores across organizations demonstrate the means to be near to the theoretical means on 9-point scales in that they are around 3 to 5 for most of the scales. This is important in that it allows the scales to reflect real changes in the climate. Many rating scales produce means heavily skewed to one end of the scale, which makes it difficult to detect changes in the skewed direction.

170

In an unpublished study at the London Business School, Dale et al. (1973) used eight of the scales of the BOCI in a longitudinal evaluation of a change programme in a manufacturing organization employing 8,500 people. The scales were administered to a random but hierarchically structured sample of managers and supervisors at three points during two years. Significant differences were shown on three of the scales over the two years, but the largest mean difference was 0·8 of a scale point. Whilst disappointing from the change agent's point of view, it provides a severe test of the test–retest reliability of the scales and they come out well.

In our survey of organizational structure and organizational climate (Payne and Pugh, 1976), we reviewed the studies reported here and others relevant, and concluded that '. . . relationships between perceived structure measures have been more reliable than relationships between climate measures'. This no doubt reflects the nebulous nature of climate as a concept, and the fact that the same climate might be produced by different values, behaviours and structures. Our facet analysis would suggest that these subjective measures of structure and climate are quite close conceptually, but the degree of closeness clearly depends on the content of the climate measures. Dimensions of centralization, for example, seem to relate more strongly to climate variables than do the structuring dimensions.

The biggest question mark about measures of climate is the one raised by Guion (1973) concerning whether or not the mean is an adequate indicator of the climate, or whether 90 per cent of the population need to endorse or fail to endorse the items before they can be considered to represent the organization. We consider that this is too harsh a criterion, but that variances and other measures of dispersion of views (as presented in Chapter 9) will give a more accurate picture of the variety of perceptions that complex organizations inevitably produce. Conceptual clarity and acknowledged complexity seem the bywords to a clearer understanding of the dimensions and determinants of organization climates.

This survey of the reliability of the measures used at the group and individual level of analysis would suggest that the role and group measures seem to have acceptable reliability and validity. Climate measures are more dubious. There is some evidence of reliability, but more work is required to see if it is the measures which are invalid, whether we have missed the variables which determine climate, or whether the determining variables are too idiosyncratic to be captured by studies of this kind.

Percentage of predictable variance as a criterion of evaluation

It is often said that science is about prediction with the idea that the ability to predict is associated with the ability to control, and that the ability to control leads to being able to assist with making decisions about the everyday world. The ability to predict, of course, depends on the reliability and validity of the measures available. In Volume II it was demonstrated that the Aston measures of Context and Structure have good reliability and validity with the exception of the centralization measures. This is reflected in the fact that, taking the four factors of structure as dependent variables, we can predict about 50 per cent of the variance from the contextual factors alone. The remaining variance is due to errors in measurement and to the choices and preferences that different managers have about how to build their organization's control structures; what Child (1972b) called 'strategic choice'.

As we have seen, the reliance on subjective perceptions reduced the reliability and validity of measures due to the distortions caused by different experiences, values, motivations and abilities of the individuals providing the data. Thus the average level of correlation between the objective measures of structure and the subjective measures of role structure is about 0·4, giving about 16 per cent of the predictable variance. The objective measures of structure predict the subjective role climate variables at about 0·2, accounting for 4 per cent of the predictable variance. The subjective measures of role structure predict the subjective role climate variables at about 0·33, accounting for about 10 per cent of the variance. Ellis and Child (Chapter 4) have shown that personality variables such as preference for a varied working environment also predict perceptions of role climate, so a start has been made on tracking down the factors that influence perceptions, but clearly much more needs to be done to find out what influences the way a senior manager sees his role. Since the design of roles lies at the heart of the design of effective organizations, and the physical and mental well-being of the managers in the organization, then the problems seem worthwhile pursuing.

As we indicated in the papers about organizational climate, the number of statistically significant correlations above chance is rather small. Typically, structural variables and hierarchical level account for perhaps 7 or 8 per cent of the variance in the climate measures. Payne and Mansfield (1975) have also shown that individual factors such as level of pay and level of job satisfaction influence the individual's perceptions of the climate and other personality and need variables will no doubt too. These add to our knowledge, but the global concept of climate seems to have the weakest support empirically. As Tagiuri (1968) observes, however, climate's appeal as a concept is that it is global, and that it is something the ordinary man can grasp. It is possible that the units to which the concept is applied may need to be smaller (groups/departments/political cliques instead of whole organizations) so as validly to describe the system as having *a* climate, but it is such a common sense analytical tool that its conceptual robustness may be worth its empirical weaknesses. The latter are, of course, a challenge too and we hope that greater attention to variance measures in analysis (as in Chapter 9) will illuminate its empirical complexity.

Common sense and evaluation

Scientific and systematic study is in the business of refining and adding to the 'common sense' knowledge from which we all start. Another way of evaluating the studies described in this volume, therefore, is to ask whether or not they have taken us beyond a common sense understanding of behaviour in organizations.

In a sense the first hypotheses that social scientists propose about a new field of study are common sense hypotheses. Bigger means more complex. More rules and regulations means less risk-taking. Bureaucracy is bad for people. One obvious improvement in our common sense knowledge is that bureaucracy is certainly not inevitably bad. Indeed, the consistent finding in these studies is that structuring of activities, whether measured objectively or subjectively, is not related to low innovation at the role level, nor to impotent group behaviour, nor to climates which stifle initiative, show little interest in scientific and technical matters, readiness to innovate, etc. And far from turning everybody into rule-abiding, don't rock the boat, compromisers, actually may be associated with increased interpersonal conflict (Child, Chapter 3).

Something else which is common to all these papers, and not so common in common sense thinking, is that things are much more complex than we thought. And this complexity is revealed by the process of trying to develop measures which allow the comparison of large numbers of organizations, roles and groups. For in that way we find examples of organizations where the bureaucracy is so well developed that it is bad, as well as organizations like 'Aston' which seem to have developed just the right amount of it to function really effectively. We also find organizations like 'Brum' which have resisted bureaucratic tendencies in order to sustain their close interpersonal relationships, but in rewarding their members for their efforts have created a lengthy hierarchical chain which is more divisive than the rules and standard procedures they have sought to avoid.

That is, it is all a matter of degree. In itself this is a common sense thought, even a truism, but the value of measurement, even if it is crude, is that it begins to permit us to discover just where the degree of one variable becomes too much for the system *given the degrees on other variables*. It is, of course, this matter of degree in regard to many interacting variables which makes it difficult to account for much of the variance in major organizational parameters. And it is because we can account for so little of the variance that our predictions about any single organization are so poor. It is this poverty in prediction about *particular* problems which leads some managers, and some social scientists, to reject this sort of approach to the study of organizations.

The ethnomethodologists, for example, argue that such broad brush approaches capture too little of the actual meanings that people place on the world of work and that it is these meanings that ultimately dictate their actual behaviour. This we wholly endorse, but some of those meanings are common amongst members of organizations and they are so partly because of the structures created. The studies here show that some of the variance in the meanings of roles and climates is predicted from a knowledge of the structure which helps to define those roles. Thus, as the Aston group has always said (Pugh et al., 1963), processual studies will benefit from taking place within a framework of structural knowledge so that organizations can be carefully selected to compare processes and meanings that arise within them on the basis of known similarities and differences in their broader structures and production technologies. Is not that itself common sense?

Further developments

If the above belief is common sense, it appears not to be common practice. There is only a handful of studies of roles or groups in organizations where the organizations have been selected on the basis of known and measured differences in structure or context and where the differences were chosen so as to test hypotheses about the effects of organizational level variables on group or role behaviour. (This comment excludes studies which merely compare different industries or large with small organizations, etc.)

We consider that there is a need to continue survey studies within the

174

comparative tradition, using a 'nested' view of organizational functioning as presented in Figure I of the Introduction, where different levels of analysis can be interrelated.

But it must be admitted that there are difficulties. Large scale comparative studies require considerable resources of people and money that are becoming more difficult to obtain. Managers in organizations are becoming more dubious of co-operating merely on an altruistic basis and demanding that research be defined in a way which is directly relevant to the organization's needs. Social scientists are moving towards a more phenomenological approach to behaviour at work.

Even so, it is the case that the work done so far can be developed within newer research contexts. Small scale comparative studies focusing on meanings and processes will surely lead to new insights and information if they are designed with reference to systematic comparisons of known organizational properties such as can be measured with the Aston schedules for organizations, roles, groups and climates at any of these levels. Cook and Campbell (1976) encourage us to take advantage of natural experiments that occur, such as when changes are made in different sites in organizations, or when they have to be made at different times for different departments. Such quasi-experiments will also benefit from selecting the sites because they have differences in structures, climates and so on, and the present measures can be used in such a selection process. In-depth studies can then be done in the context of these structural, technological, performance and cultural differences. If the studies also turn out to be longitudinal, then standard measures of these kinds can help detect changes which occur over time. The detection of such changes will raise questions that will test the validity of the processual data that is more in demand today. This route of competing, but also interacting, approaches, is the surest path to the cognitive refinement and greater understanding for which we all aim.

Bibliography

Allen, T.J. and Cohen, S.I., 1969, 'Information flow in research and development laboratories', *Administrative Science Quarterly,* vol. 4, no. 1, pp. 12-20.

Argyris, C., 1957, *Personality and Organization,* Harper, New York.

Argyris, C., 1960, *Understanding Organizational Behavior,* Tavistock, London.

Argyris, C., 1964, *Integrating the Individual and the Organization,* Tavistock, London.

Barker, R.G., 1965, 'Explorations in ecological psychology', *American Psychologist,* vol. 20, pp. 1-14.

Barker, R.G., 1968, *Ecological Psychology,* Stanford University Press, Stanford, California.

Barnes, L.B., 1960, *Organizational Systems and Engineering Groups,* Harvard Business School, Boston.

Bennis, Warren G., 1959, 'Leadership Theory and Administrative Behavior: the Problem of Authority', *Administrative Science Quarterly,* vol. 4, pp. 259-301.

Berkowitz, N.W. and Bennis, W.G., 1961, 'Interaction patterns in formal service orientated organizations', *Administrative Science Quarterly,* vol. 6, no. 2, pp. 25-50.

Berrien, F.K., 1967, 'A general systems approach to social taxonomy' in B.P. Indik and F.K. Berrien (eds), *People, Groups and Organizations,* Teachers College Press, New York.

Blau, P.M., 1955, *The Dynamics of Bureaucracy,* University Press, Chicago.

Blau, P.M. and Schoenherr, R.A., 1971, *The Structure of Organizations,* Basic Books, New York.

Brech, E.F.L., 1957, *Organization: the Framework of Management,* Longman Green, London.

Brogden, H.E., 1949, 'A new coefficient: applications to biserial correlations and to estimation of selective efficiency', *Psychometrika,* vol. 14, pp. 169-82.

Brown, W., 1960, *Exploration in Management,* Heinemann, London.

Burns, T., 1954, 'The directions of activity and communication in a departmental executive group', *Human Relations,* vol. 7, pp. 73-97.

Burns, T., 1963, 'Industry in a New Age', *New Society,* vol. 18, January, pp. 17-20.

Burns, T. and Stalker, G.M., 1961, *The Management of Innovation,* Tavistock, London.

Burrage, M., 1969, 'Culture and British Economic Growth', *British Journal of Sociology,* vol. 20, pp. 117–33.

Campbell, J.P., Dunette, M.D., Lawler, E.E. and Weick, K.E., 1970, *Managerial Behaviour, Performance and Effectiveness,* McGraw-Hill, New York.

Child, J., 1972a, 'Organization Structure and Strategies of Control', *Administrative Science Quarterly,* vol. 17, pp. 163–77. (Reprinted in Pugh and Hinings, 1976.)

Child, J., 1972b, 'Organizational Structure, Environment and Performance: the Role of Strategic Choice', *Sociology,* vol. 6, pp. 1–22.

Child, J., 1973 'Predicting and Understanding Organizational Structure', *Administrative Science Quarterly,* vol. 18, pp. 168–75. (Reprinted in Pugh and Hinings, 1976.)

Child, J. and Ellis, T., 1973, 'Predictors of Variation in Managerial Roles', *Human Relations,* vol. 26, no. 2, pp. 227–50.

Child, J. and Mansfield, R., 1972 'Technology, Size and Organization Structure', *Sociology,* vol. 6, pp. 369–93.

Cook, T.D. and Campbell, D.T., 1976, 'The Design and Conduct of Quasi-experiments and True Experiments in Field Settings', in M.D. Dunnette (ed.), *Handbook of Industrial and Organizational Psychology,* Rand McNally, Chicago.

Crozier, M., 1964, *The Bureaucratic Phenomenon,* Tavistock, London.

Cummings, L.L. and El Salmi, A.M., 1968, 'Empirical Research on the Bases and Correlates of Managerial Motivation', *Psychological Bulletin,* vol. 70, pp. 127–44.

Dale, A.J., Payne, R.L., McMillan, B. and Pym, D., 1973, 'Evaluation of a 3-D Theory of Organizational Change', Unpublished report, London Graduate School of Business Studies.

Dubin, R., 1970, 'Management in Britain: Impressions of a Visiting Professor', *Journal of Management Studies,* vol. 7, no. 2, pp. 182–98.

Fayol, H., 1949, *General and Industrial Management,* Pitman, London.

Fiedler, F.E., 1971, 'Validation and Extension of the Contingency Model of Leadership Effectiveness: a Review of Empirical Findings', *Psychological Bulletin,* vol. 76, pp. 128–48.

Foa, U.G., 1965, 'New developments in facet design and analysis', *Psychological Review,* vol. 72, no. 4, pp. 262–74.

Frank, A. Gunder, 1963–4, 'Administrative Role Definition and Social Changes', *Human Organization,* vol. 22, Winter, pp. 238–42.

Friedlander, F., 1970, 'The relationships of task and human conditions to effective organizational structure' in Bernard Bass et al. (eds), *Managing for Accomplishment,* pp. 111–39, Lexington Books, Lexington, Mass.

Gordon, G. and Becker, S., 1964, 'Changes in Medical Practice Bring Shifts in Patterns of Power', *The Modern Hospital,* vol. 102, February.

Gorman, L. and Malloy, E., 1972, *People, Jobs and Organizations,* Irish Management Institution.

Gouldner, A.W., 1955, *Patterns of Industrial Bureaucracy,* Routledge and Kegan Paul, London.

Gouldner, A.W., 1957, 'Cosmopolitans and locals: towards an analysis of latent social roles', *Administrative Science Quarterly,* vol. 2, pp. 281–306.

Gross, N., Mason W. and McEachern, A., 1958, *Explorations in Role Analysis.* Wiley, New York.

Guetzkow, G., 1965, 'Communications in Organizations', in J.G. March (ed.), *Handbook of Organizations,* Rand McNally, Chicago.

Guilford, J.P., 1954, *Psychometric Methods,* McGraw-Hill, New York.

Guilford, J.P., 1956, *Fundamental Statistics in Psychology and Education,* McGraw-Hill, New York.

Guion, R.M., 1973, 'A Note on Organizational Climate', *Organizational Behaviour and Human Performance,* vol. 9, no. 1, pp. 120–5.

Gulick, L. and Urwick, L., 1937, *Papers on the Sciences of Administration,* Institute of Public Administration, New York.

Guttman, L., 1954, 'An outline of some new methodology in social research', *Public Opinion Quarterly,* vol. 18, pp. 395–404.

Hage, J., 1965, 'An Axiomatic Theory of Organizations', *Administrative Science Quarterly,* vol. 10, pp. 289–320.

Hage, J. and Aiken, M., 1967, 'Relationships of Centralization to other Structural Properties', *Administrative Science Quarterly,* vol. 12, pp. 72–92.

Hall, R.H., 1962, 'Intraorganizational Structural Variation: application of the Bureaucratic Model', *Administrative Science Quarterly,* vol. 7, pp. 295–308.

Hall, R.H., 1963, 'The concept of bureaucracy: an empirical assessment', *American Journal of Sociology,* vol. 69, pp. 32–40.

Harrington, A., 1960, *Life in the "Crystal Palace",* Cape, London.

Hart, P. and Mellors, J., 1970, 'Management Youth and Company Growth: a Correlation?', *Management Decision,* vol. 4, no. 1, pp. 50–2.

Hemphill, J.K., 1956, 'Group Dimensions: a Manual for their Measurement', Working Paper, Columbus Ohio State University Bureau of

Business Research, Research Monograph no. 87.

Hickson, D.J., 1966, 'A Convergence in Organization Theory', *Administrative Science Quarterly,* vol. 11, pp. 225–37. (Chapter 1 of this book.)

Hickson, D.J. and Macdonald, K.M., 1964, 'A Scheme for the Empirical Study of Organizational Behaviour', *The International Journal of Production Research,* vol. 3, pp. 29–34.

Hickson, D.J. and Pugh, D.S., 1965, 'The Facts about Bureaucracy', *The Manager,* December, pp. 37–40.

Hickson, D.J., Pugh, D.S. and Pheysey, D.C., 1969, 'Operations Technology and Organizational Structure: an Empirical Reappraisal', *Administrative Science Quarterly,* vol. 14, pp. 378–97. (Reprinted in Pugh and Hickson, 1976.)

Hinings, C.R. et al., 1967 'An approach to the study of Bureaucracy', *Sociology,* vol. 1, pp. 62–72. (see Chapter 2 of Pugh and Hickson, 1976.)

Hubbel, C.H., 1965, 'An input-output approach to clique identification', *Sociometry,* vol. 28, pp. 276–97.

Indik, B.P., 1963, 'Some effects of organization size on member attitudes and behavior', *Human Relations,* vol. 16, pp. 360–84.

Inkson, J.H.K., Hickson, D.J. and Pugh, D.S., 1968, 'Administrative Reduction of Variance in Organization and Behaviour: a Comparative Study', British Psychological Society Conference Paper. (Chapter 2 of this book.)

Inkson, J.H.K., Payne, R.L. and Pugh, D.S., 1967, 'Extending the Occupational Environment: the Measurement of Organizations', *Occupational Psychology,* vol. 41, pp. 33–47.

Inkson, J.H.K., Pugh, D.S. and Hickson, D.J., 1970, 'Organization Context and Structure: an abbreviated replication', *Administrative Science Quarterly,* vol. 15, pp. 318–29. (Reprinted in Pugh and Hinings, 1976.)

Inkson, J.H.K. et al., 1970, 'A Comparison of Organization Structure and Managerial Roles, Ohio U.S.A. and the Midlands England', *Journal of Management Studies,* vol. 7, no. 3, pp. 347–63.

Inkson, J.H.K., Schwitter, J.P., Pheysey, D.C. and Hickson, D.J., 1971, *Comparison of Birmingham, England and Ohio, U.S.A. Organizations,* Working Paper, University of Aston in Birmingham.

Janowitz, M., 1959, 'Changing Patterns of Organizational Authority: the Military Establishment', *Administrative Science Quarterly,* vol. 3, pp. 473–93.

Jaques, E., 1961, *Equitable Payment,* Heinemann, London.

Kahn, R.L., Wolfe, D.M., Quinn, R.P., Snoek, J.D. and Rosenthal, R.A., 1964, *Organizational Stress: Studies in Role Conflict and Ambiguity,* Wiley, New York.

Kammerer, G.M., 1964, 'Role Diversity of City Managers', *Administrative Science Quarterly,* vol. 8, pp. 421–42.

Katz, L., 1953, 'A new status index derived from sociometric analysis', *Psychometrika,* vol. 18, pp. 39–43.

Katz, D. and Kahn, R.L., 1966, *The Social Psychology of Organizations,* Wiley, New York.

Kohn, M.L., 1971, 'Bureaucratic Man: a portrait and an interpretation', *American Sociological Review,* vol. 36, pp. 461–74.

Landsberger, H.A., 1961, 'Horizontal dimensions in bureaucracy', *Administrative Science Quarterly,* vol. 6, pp. 299–332.

Levinson, D.J., 1959, 'Role, Personality and Social Structure in the Organizational Setting', *Journal of Abnormal and Social Psychology,* vol. 58, March, pp. 170–81.

Levy, P. and Pugh, D.S., 1969, 'Scaling and Multivariate Analyses in the Study of Organizational Variables', *Sociology,* vol. 3, pp. 193–213. (Reprinted in Pugh and Hickson, 1976.)

Lewin, K., 1951, *Field Theory in Social Sciences,* Harper, New York.

Likert, K., 1961, *New Patterns of Management,* McGraw-Hill, New York.

Litwak, E., 1961, 'Models of Bureaucracy which permit Conflict', *American Journal of Sociology,* vol. 67, pp. 177–84.

Litwin, G.H. and Stringer, R.A., 1968, *Motivation and Organizational Climate,* Harvard University, Cambridge.

Mace, C.A., 1952, 'Education for Management in the United States: some impressions and reflections', *Occupational Psychology,* vol. 26, pp. 61–9.

McGegor, D., 1960, *The Human Side of Enterprise,* McGraw-Hill, New York.

McLennan, K., 1967, 'The Manager and his Job Skills', *Academy of Management Journal,* vol. 1, pp. 235–45.

McMurry, R.N., 1958, 'Recruitment, Dependency and Morale in the Banking Industry', *Administrative Science Quarterly,* vol. 3, pp. 87–106.

March, J.G. and Simon, H.A., 1958, *Organizations,* Wiley, New York.

Melman, S., 1958, *Decision-Making and Productivity,* Blackwell, Oxford.

Merton, R.K., 1940, 'Bureaucratic Structure and Personality', *Social Forces,* vol. 17, pp. 560–8.

Millerson, C.L., 1964, *The Qualifying Associations,* Routledge and Kegan Paul, London.

Moreno, J.L. and Jennings, H.H., 1938, 'Statistics of Social Configuration', *Sociometry,* vol. 1, pp. 342-74.

Murray, Henry, 1938, *Explorations in Personality,* Oxford University Press, New York.

Pace, C.R., 1963, *College and University Environment Scales,* Educational Testing Service, Princeton, NJ.

Pace, C.R., 1966, *Comparison of College and University Environment Scales: Results from Different Groups of Reporters,* Educational Testing Service, Princeton, NJ.

Payne, R.L., Fineman, S. and Wall, T.D., 1976, 'Organizational Climate and Job Satisfaction: a Conceptual Synthesis', *Organizational Behaviour and Human Performance,* vol. 16, pp. 45-62.

Payne, R.L. and Mansfield, Roger, 1973, 'Relationships of Perceptions of Organizational Climate to Organizational Structure, Context, and Hierarchical Position', *Administrative Science Quarterly,* vol. 18, pp. 515-26. (Edited extracts form Chapter 8 of this book.)

Payne, Roy, and Mansfield, Roger, 1975, 'Some Correlates of Individuals' Perceptions of Organization Climate', MRC Social and Applied Psychology Unit, Sheffield, Working Paper no. 58.

Payne, R.L. and Pheysey, D.C., 1971, 'Organizational Structure and Sociometric Choice amongst Line Managers in three Contrasted Organizations', *European Journal of Social Psychology,* vol. 1, pp. 261-84. (Chapter 6 in this book.)

Payne, R.L. and Pheysey, D.C., 1971, 'Stern's Organizational Climate Index: a Reconceptualization and Application to Business Organizations', *Organizational Behavior and Human Performance,* vol. 6, no. 1, pp. 77-98. (Chapter 7 in this book.)

Payne, R.L. and Pugh, D.S., 1971, 'Organizations as Psychological Environments', in Peter Warr (ed.) *Psychology at Work,* Penguin Books.

Payne, R.L. and Pugh, D.S., 1976, 'Organizational Structure and Climate' in M. Dunnette (ed.), *Handbook of Organizational Psychology,* Rand-McNally, Chicago.

Pervin, L.A., 1968, 'Performance and Satisfaction as a function of individual environment fit', *Psychological Bulletin,* vol. 69, pp. 56-68.

Pheysey, D.C. and Payne, R.L., 1970, 'The Hemphill Group Dimensions Description Questionnaire: a British Industrial Application', *Human Relations,* vol. 23, pp. 473-97.

Pheysey, D.C., Payne, R.L. and Pugh, D.S., 1971, 'Influence of

Structure at Organizational and Group Levels', *Administrative Science Quarterly,* vol. 16, pp. 61–73. (An edited version forms Chapter 5 in this book.)

Platt, Jennifer, 1976, *Realities of Social Research: an Empirical Study on British Sociologists,* Sussex University Press, Brighton.

Porter, L.W., 1963, 'Where is the Organization Man?', *Harvard Business Review,* vol. 41, pp. 53–61.

Porter, L.W. and Lawler, E.E., 1965, 'Properties of Organization Structure in Relation to Job Attitudes and Job Behavior', *Psychological Bulletin,* vol. 64, pp. 23–51.

Presthus, R.V., 1958, 'Toward a Theory of Organizational Behaviour', *Administrative Science Quarterly,* vol. 3, pp. 48–77.

Pugh, D.S., Hickson, D.J., Hinings, C.R., Macdonald, K.M., Turner, C. and Lupton, T., 1963, 'A Conceptual Scheme for Organizational Analysis', *Administrative Science Quarterly,* vol. 8, pp. 289–315. (Reprinted in Pugh and Hickson, 1976.)

Pugh, D.S., Hickson, D.J., Hinings, C.R. and Turner, C., 1968, 'Dimensions of Organizational Structure', *Administrative Science Quarterly,* vol. 13, pp. 65–105. (Reprinted in Pugh and Hickson, 1976.)

Pugh, D.S., Hickson, D.J., Hinings, C.R. and Turner, C., 1969, 'The Context of Organization Structure', *Administrative Science Quarterly,* vol. 14, pp. 91–114. (Reprinted in Pugh and Hickson, 1976.)

Pugh, D.S. and Hickson, D.J., 1976, *Organizational Structure in its Context, The Aston Programme I,* Saxon House/Lexington Books.

Pugh, D.S. and Hinings, C.R., 1976, *Organizational Structure: Extensions and Replications, The Aston Programme II,* Saxon House/Lexington Books.

Pugh, D.S., Inkson, J.H.K. and Levy, P.M., 1966, 'The Scaling of Variables in the Work Environment', Paper presented to the British Psychological Society Annual Conference.

Pym, D., 1966, 'Technology, Effectiveness and Pre-disposition Towards Work Changes amongst Mechanical Engineers', *Journal of Management Studies,* vol. 3, pp. 304–11.

Pym, D., 1966, 'Effective Managerial Performance in Organizational Changes', *Journal of Management Studies,* vol. 3, no. 1, pp. 73–84.

Pym, D., 1968, 'Organization Evaluation and Management Training', *Journal of Management Studies,* vol. 5, no. 2, pp. 167–182.

Seashore, S.E., 1954, *Group Cohesiveness in the Industrial Work Group,* University of Michigan Press, Ann Arbor.

Schein, E.H., 1970, *Organizational Psychology,* Prentice-Hall, Englewood Cliffs, NJ.

Schneider, B., 1972, 'Organizational Climate: individual preferences and organizational realities,' *Journal of Applied Psychology,* vol. 56, pp. 211-17.

Sells, S.B., 1963, 'Dimensions of Stimulus situations which account for Behavior Variance' in S.B. Sells (ed.) *Stimulus Determinants of Behavior,* Ronald Press, New York.

Selznick, P., 1957, *Leadership in Administration,* Row Peterson, Evanston, Ill.

Shaw, Marvin E., 1963, 'Scaling Group Tasks: a method for dimensional analysis', Working Paper, University of Florida Technical Report no. 1.

Simon, H.A., 1960, *The New Science of Management Decisions,* Harper, New York.

Simon, H.A., 1962, 'The Architecture of Complexity', *Proceedings of the American Philosophical Society,* vol. 106, pp. 467-82.

Smith, Patricia C., Kendall, L.M. and Hulin, C.L., 1969, *The Measurement of Satisfaction in Work and Retirement,* Rand-McNally, Chicago.

Stern, G.C., 1967, *People in Context: the Measurement of Environmental Interaction in School and Society,* vol. 1, unpublished report, Library of the University of Syracuse.

Stern, G.G., 1970, *People in Context,* Wiley, New York.

Stern, G.G., Stein, M.I. and Bloom, B.S., 1956, *Methods in Personality Assessment,* Free Press, Glencoe, Ill.

Stogdill, R.M., 1951, 'The Organization of Working Relationships: Twenty Sociometric Indices', *Sociometry,* vol. 14, pp. 366-73.

Stogdill, R.M., 1959, *Individual Behavior in Group Achievement: a Theory,* Oxford University Press, New York.

Sullivan, H.S., 1953, *The Interpersonal Theory of Psychiatry,* Norton, New York.

Tagiuri, R., 1968, 'Executive Climate' in R. Tagiuri and G.H. Litwin (eds), *Organizational Climate: Explorations of a Concept,* Harvard University, Cambridge.

Taylor, F.W., 1947, *Scientific Management,* Harper, New York.

Thomas, E.J., 1959, 'Role Conceptions and Organizational Size', *American Sociological Review,* vol. 24, pp. 30-7.

Thompson, V.A., 1965, 'Bureaucracy and Innovation', *Administrative Science Quarterly,* vol. 10, pp. 1-20.

Tunstall, J., 1964, *The Advertising Man,* Chapman and Hall.

Udy, S., 1965, 'The Comparative Analysis of Organizations', in J.G. March (ed.), *Handbook of Organizations,* pp. 678–809, Rand-McNally, Chicago.

Urwick, L.F., 1947, *The Elements of Administration,* Pitman, London.

Vroom, V.H., 1964, *Work and Motivation,* Wiley, New York.

Weber, M., 1946, *Essays in Sociology,* ed. by H.H. Gerth and C. Wright Mills, Oxford University Press, New York.

Weber, M., 1947, *The Theory of Social and Economic Organization,* Free Press, Glencoe, Ill.

Weiss, R.S. and Jacobson, E., 1955, 'A Method for the Analysis of the Structure of Complex Organizations', *American Sociological Review,* vol. 20, pp. 668–70.

Whyte, W.F., 1948, 'Incentives for Productivity: the Bundy Tubing Company Case', *Applied Anthropology,* vol. 7, pp. 1–16.

Whyte, W.F., 1960, *The Organization Man,* Penguin, Harmondsworth.

Woodward, J., 1965, *Industrial Organization: Theory and Practice,* Oxford University Press, London.

Names index

Subject index

187

The editors

Derek Pugh and Roy Payne were both formerly members of the Industrial Administration Research Unit at the University of Aston in Birmingham. Professor Pugh is now Professor of Organizational Behaviour at the London Graduate School of Business Studies, and Dr Payne is with the Medical Research Council's Social and Applied Psychology Unit at Sheffield University.

Other SAXON HOUSE publications

Hopwood, A. G. — *An accounting system and managerial behaviour*

Black, I. G., et al — *Advanced urban transport*

Pollock, N. C. — *Animals, environment and man in Africa*

McLean, A. T. — *Business and accounting in Europe*

Rogers, S. J., B. H. Davey — *The common agricultural policy and Britain*

Hermet, G. — *The communists in Spain*

Klingen, J. S. — *Company strategy*

Chrzanowski, I. — *Concentration and centralisation of capital in shipping*

Bailey, R. V., J. Young (eds) — *Contemporary social problems in Britain*

Mack, J. A. — *The crime industry*

Sjølund, A. — *Daycare institutions and children's development*

Lewis, C. — *Demand analysis and inventory control*

Jambrek, P. — *Development and social change in Yugoslavia*

Macmillan, J. — *Deviant drivers*

Richards, M. G., M. E. Ben-Akiva — *A disaggregate travel demand model*

Teff, H. — *Drugs, society and the law*

Snickers, F. et al (eds) — *Dynamic allocation of urban space*

Ellison, A. P., E. M. Stafford — *The dynamics of the civil aviation industry*

Birnbaum, K. E. — *East and West Germany*

Masnata, A. — *East-West economic co-operation*

Ghosh, D. — *The economics of building societies*

Richardson, H. W. — *The economics of urban size*

Starkie, D. N., D. M. Johnson — *The economic value of peace and quiet*

John, I. G. (ed.) — *EEC policy towards Eastern Europe*

More, W. S. (ed.) — *Emotions and adult learning*

Grassman, S. — *Exchange reserves and the financial structure of foreign trade*

Thompson, M. S. — *Evaluation for decision in social programmes*

von Geusau, F.A.M.A. (ed.) — *The external relations of the European Community*

Bergmann, T. — *Farm policies in socialist countries*

Ash, J. C. K., D. J. Smyth — *Forecasting the U.K. economy*

Blank, S. — *Government and industry in Britain*

Buttler, F. A. — *Growth pole theory and economic development*

Richardson, H. W., et al — *Housing and urban spatial structure*

van Duijn, J. J. — *An interregional model of economic fluctuations*

Brittain, J. M., S. A. Roberts (eds) — *Inventory of information resources in the social sciences*

Fukuda, H. — *Japan and world trade*

Jackson, M. P. — *Labour relations on the docks*

Stephenson, I. S. — *The law relating to agriculture*

Hess, H. — *Mafia and Mafiosi*

Vodopivec, K. — *Maladjusted youth*

Hovell, P. J., et al — *The management of urban public transport*

Funnell, B. M., R. D. Hey (eds) — *The management of water resources in England and Wales*

Martin, M. J. C. — *Management science and urban problems*

Rhenman, E. — *Managing the community hospital*

Giddings, P. J. — *Marketing boards and ministers*

Klaassen, L. H., P. Drewe — *Migration policy in Europe*

Chapman, C. B. — *Modular decision analysis*